Mitchell Symons was born in London and educated at Mill Hill School and the LSE, where he studied law. Since leaving BBC TV, where he was a researcher and then a director, he has worked as a writer, broadcaster and journalist. He was a principal writer of early editions of the board game Trivial Pursuit and has devised many television formats. He is also the author of more than thirty books, and currently writes a weekly column for the *Sunday Express*.

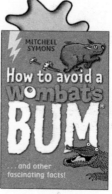

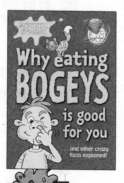

MITCHELL SYMONS

Do Igloos Have LOOS?

and other cool questions answered!

DOUBLEDAY

DO IGLOOS HAVE LOOS?
A DOUBLEDAY BOOK 978 0 385 61784 0

Published in Great Britain by Doubleday,
an imprint of Random House Children's Books
A Random House Group Company

This edition published 2010

1 3 5 7 9 10 8 6 4 2

[The Random House Group Limited supports the Forest Stewardship Council
(FSC), the leading international forest certification organization. All our titles
that are printed on Greenpeace-approved FSC-certified paper carry the FSC
logo. Our paper procurement policy can be found at www.rbooks.co.uk/
environment.]

Mixed Sources
Product group from well-managed
forests and other controlled sources
FSC   www.fsc.org Cert no. TT-COC-2139
© 1996 Forest Stewardship Council

RANDOM HOUSE CHILDREN'S BOOKS
61–63 Uxbridge Road, London W5 5SA

www.kidsatrandomhouse.co.uk
www.rbooks.co.uk

Addresses for companies within The Random House Group Limited can be
found at: www.randomhouse.co.uk/offices.htm

THE RANDOM HOUSE GROUP Limited Reg. No. 954009

A CIP catalogue record for this book is available from the British Library.

Printed and bound in Great Britain by Clays Ltd, St Ives plc

To my wonderful sisters, Jenny and Gilly.
If they are – as I always tell them they are
– the Ugly Sisters, then I guess that makes
me Cinderella.
What a bizarre thought!

This is the seventh book in a series that started with *How to Avoid a Wombat's Bum*. But, within those seven books, it's also the third of a question-and-answer trilogy. The first of those three books was *Why Eating Bogeys Is Good for You*, which was one of the 12 books chosen by the Government's 'Booked Up' scheme to be offered free to all pupils in Year Seven. It also won the Blue Peter 'Best Book with Facts' Award 2010.

It turned out to be the most successful, and although that was possibly because of the silly title, I think readers were genuinely interested to know the answers to questions like *Do identical twins have identical fingerprints?*, *Do two wrongs make a right?*, *What happens to a cow if you don't milk it?*, *Why would anyone want to pop a weasel?*, and, yes, *Is eating bogeys bad for you?*

The next book in this question-and-answer series-within-a-series was *Why Do Farts Smell Like Rotten Eggs?* (and, please remember, I only write 'em – I don't give 'em their titles!). This contained such questions as *Why does vomit always contain carrots?*, *Has anyone ever been rescued after sending a message in a bottle?*, *Why shouldn't you be able to have your cake and eat it?* and *Why is flu called flu?*

I thought that two books would cover all the unanswered (and unanswerable) questions in the known universe.

How wrong could I be?

No sooner had *Farts* (as my editor and I tend to refer to the second of these three books) come out than I was getting emails from readers asking me to answer questions it hadn't even occurred to me to ask. Then friends started getting in on the act. 'Hey, Mitch, great book,' they'd start off, before – inevitably – going on to say, 'But you didn't answer the question that's always fascinated me . . .' Sometimes it would just be silly (like *How long's a piece of string?*) or personally rude (like *Have you ever considered saying 'no' when you're offered seconds at dinner?*), but at other times I'd get some real humdingers that made me want to rush off and find out the answers.

Yup, that's the sort of man I am.

Once again, where possible, I went to experts for the answers. My thanks to them all. I also, of course, used my large library of reference books as well as the Internet (although I tried to use this to check facts rather than, as is so tempting, as a tool of first resort).

Now for some even more important acknowledgements, because without these people this book couldn't have been written at all: (in alphabetical order) my fabulous editor, Lauren Buckland; my wife and chief researcher, Penny Chorlton; my publisher, Annie Eaton; the designers, Dominica Jonscher and Nigel Baines.

In addition, I'd also like to thank the following people for their help, contributions and/or support: Gilly Adams, Luigi Bonomi, Paul Donnelley, Jonathan Fingerhut, Jenny Garrison, Bryn Musson, Nicholas Ridge, Mari Roberts, Charlie Symons, Jack Symons, Louise Symons, David Thomas, Martin Townsend and Rob Woolley.

If I've missed anyone out, then please know that – as with any mistakes in the book – it is, as I always say, entirely down to my own stupidity.

Mitchell Symons, 2010
www.mitchellsymons.co.uk

Who made the very first map of the world?

It was a man named Anaximander, who was a sixth-century BC Greek philosopher. He drew up his map to help navigation and trade and to help persuade the Ionian states to join a federation. But they weren't the only reasons: he was also driven by the fascination of producing a map – for the sake of knowledge itself. Interestingly, he was not only the first geographer; he was also the founder of astronomy and is credited with inventing the sundial. Anaximander was the first person to suggest that the Earth floated unsupported in space rather than resting on turtles, elephants or a vast ocean.

WELL, THAT'S A RELIEF

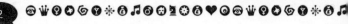

Has anyone visited every country on Earth?

It's impossible to say how many people have achieved such a feat, as they wouldn't necessarily tell anyone, but we do know that a man named Maurizio Giuliano, a graduate of both Oxford and Cambridge universities, has visited every single country in the world.

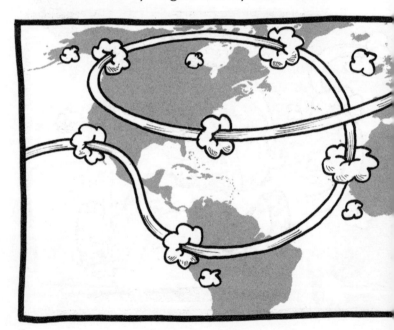

That's 193 countries!

What is more, he had achieved this feat by the age of just 29. He was 28 years and 361 days old when he went to Suriname, the last country he visited.

He says that it's possible that he might have an 'addiction to crossing borders'.

I should say so!

What is the longest 'word' you can 'write' on a calculator?

I was always impressed by my ability to 'write' SHELL OIL (71077345) and ESSO OIL (7100553) on a calculator, but after doing some research, I realize that I'm just an amateur!

Of course, most calculators only give you eight digits, but if you were to get a calculator with more digits to play with, you could do the nine-letter word ILLEGIBLE (378193771) or the 11-letter word HILLBILLIES (53177187714).

However, even better are the 12-letter words BIBLIOLOGIES (531607017818), GEOBIOLOGIES (531607018036) and GLOSSOLOGIES (531607055076).

No, I don't know what they mean either, but does it matter when they give us so much fun!

Why do the French count to 'sixty-ten' rather than to seventy?

As you might know, the French have a somewhat different – not to say daft – counting system to ours.

Below seventy, it's all very logical, but then it goes absolutely haywire!

Having come up with perfectly good words for twenty, thirty, forty, fifty and sixty, the French basically give up and call seventy 'soixante-dix' or sixty-ten. Seventy-one is 'sixty-eleven', seventy-two is 'sixty-twelve', and so on.

But the barminess doesn't stop there. They can't be bothered to come up with a word for eighty either. So what do they do instead? Yes, you've guessed it, they call it 'quatre-vingts' or 'four twenties'.

And then the plot gets lost entirely at ninety, where instead of a single word (like 'ninety' or 'neuftante'), or even an eighty-style mathematical sum (like 'three thirties'), they count up from 'four twenties-eleven'. So that by the time they get to, say, ninety-eight, they're calling it 'quatre-vingts dix-huit' (four twenties and eighteen).

That's five syllables to our three. Who knows, maybe they've got more time to spare than we have.

Why do they do it? No one seems to know, though it's worth pointing out that it's usually the oldest and most used words in any language that are the most irregular. For proof of that, just look at the way the verb 'to be' is conjugated in any language you can think of – including English.

But that doesn't answer the question.

In any event, if you ask a French person why – as I've done on more than one occasion – they'll shrug their shoulders (the French do an awful lot of shoulder-shrugging) and simply say, 'Parce que.' Which means 'because' and is therefore probably the best answer I can offer you.

Apart, that is, from a very real suspicion that they do it to confuse us.

Why is green the colour of envy?

The ancient Greeks and Romans believed that the human body was filled with four basic substances they called 'humours'. When a person was healthy, these humours were in balance. When they were ill, it was because the humours were unbalanced.

The four humours were black bile, yellow bile, phlegm and blood, and they were closely related to the four elements of earth, fire, water and air.

Jealousy or envy was considered to be the result of an excess of yellow bile, which would turn the skin a yellowish green. Therefore green became the colour of envy and jealousy – something that Shakespeare showed when he called jealousy 'the green-eyed monster' in the play *Othello*.

Is it possible to say who invented the jigsaw puzzle?

It is! It was John Spilsbury in (or around) 1767. Spilsbury was an engraver and mapmaker, and his first puzzle was a map of England and Wales. He attached a map to a piece of wood and then cut out each country with a marquetry saw. Next he made a jigsaw of the map of Europe, cutting out the pieces to fit each country's borders. He then did this for the map of the world, with a separate piece for each country.

Teachers used Spilsbury's puzzles to teach geography as students learned about countries by putting the pieces back together.

How far away is the horizon?

OK, first of all let's establish what we mean by the horizon. According to my dictionary, it's the apparent line that separates the Earth from the sky.

I think the key word there is 'apparent', because the position of the horizon is going to depend on a number of factors (such as where you are, how tall you are and how good the visibility is).

The only general rule we can even begin to make is that, generally speaking, the horizon is about three miles away – assuming you're looking across a flat plain or out to sea. After three miles, the Earth's curve makes it impossible to see further.

Of course, if you're on an elevated plain (rather than a flat one) – perhaps at the top of a cliff – then you're going to be able to see further. You can add even more distance to that as you grow taller (something to look forward to!).

Should belly-buttons go in or stick out?

Some navels (or belly-buttons) go in, while others stick out or protrude. There's no 'should' about it.

Why do vicars wear dog collars?

For a start, vicars (and other members of the clergy) don't like the term 'dog collar'; they prefer 'clerical collar'.

Right, now we've got that settled, let's get on with the answer. The dog collar – sorry, *clerical* collar – is a fairly recent introduction. It goes back to the mid 19th century, when a Roman Catholic order visited this country wearing them – just to distinguish themselves from other clergymen. By the end of the 19th century, other Christian denominations

also adopted the dog collar – sorry, *clerical* collar. This wasn't for any particular religious reason but simply to identify themselves as clergymen.

Has anyone lived in three different centuries?

That sounds extraordinary – not to say impossible – but, thinking about it, anyone born in 1899 who lived to be 102 would have made it.

So the first job is to find someone who was born in 1899, etc., etc.

Well, my grandmother, Millie – known as 'Mustn't Grumble' because whenever you asked her how she was, she'd say, 'Mustn't grumble' – was born in 1899 but, alas for the sake of this question, died in 1988.

Eventually, after no little research, I came across two people I'd like to bring to your attention.

The first is the great ballerina Dame Ninette de Valois, who was born on 6 June 1898 (in the 19th century), lived throughout the 20th century and died on 8 March 2001 (in the 21st century). She established the Royal Ballet and is regarded as one of the most influential personalities in ballet history.

The second is a man named Henry Allingham, who was born precisely two years earlier than Dame Ninette, on 6 June 1896. He not only lived throughout the 20th century; in 2009 (the year he died) he became, at the age of 113, the oldest man in the world.

He didn't get to such a monumental age by doing nothing. On the contrary, he fought in the First World War and was the last surviving founder member of the RAF. He lived to see five grandchildren, 12 great-grandchildren, 14 great-great-grandchildren and one great-great-great-grandchild.

Dame Ninette Valois and Henry Allingham: two remarkable people.

Why do people say 'as dead as a dodo' – why not as dead as some other creature?

Good question. Plenty of creatures have become extinct: why pick on the poor old dodo?

To understand why, we have to look at what happened to the dodo.

The dodo was a bird – a member of the dove family – but it was a metre tall, fat (a bit like a turkey) and, most importantly, couldn't fly.

YOU'LL NEVER GET ME UP IN ONE OF THOSE

Which meant it was a sitting duck. Or sitting dodo.

Dutch sailors were the first human predators the dodo encountered. This was in 1598, on the island of Mauritius in the Indian Ocean. Until it met these Dutchmen, the dodo had no natural enemies and therefore was incredibly trusting. Add to this the sad fact that the female dodo laid just one egg a year . . . well, you can guess the rest, can't you?

Roast dodo led to total extinction within 100 years.

And that's why we say 'as dead as a dodo'.

Who first played Snakes and Ladders?

The game of Snakes and Ladders has its origins in ancient India, where it wasn't so much a game as a religious guide to behaviour.

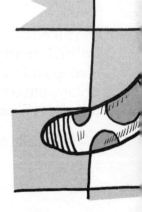

Hindu spiritual teachers used it to show children the importance of good deeds as opposed to bad deeds. The ladders represented virtues such as generosity and humility while the snakes represented vices like anger and dishonesty. So by doing good things, people could achieve salvation, but by doing bad ones, they would become reborn as a lower form of life. There were always more snakes than ladders, to show people just how hard it is to reach salvation.

As you might know, India was part of the British Empire, and in the late 19th century Snakes and Ladders was brought back to Britain, but only as a game (i.e. without any religious or moral dimensions to it).

It's still really difficult to win though!

What is the toughest creature on Earth?

My first thought is the cockroach. I say *the* cockroach, but there are some 4,000 species of cockroach. However, they're all pretty tough and *extremely* resilient. It's been said that cockroaches have adjusted to living with us much better than we have adjusted to living with them.

In fact, it's often said that cockroaches are the only creatures that would survive a nuclear war. This is actually true: scientists

have proved that cockroaches can absorb 100 times more radiation (the after-effect of a nuclear bomb) than it takes to kill a human being.

Readers of my other books will also know that cockroaches:

•can survive underwater for 15 minutes;

•detect movement as small as 2,000 times the diameter of a hydrogen atom;

•live for several weeks after being decapitated.

Add to these extraordinary facts that, if a cockroach breaks a leg, it can grow another

one, and that it's the fastest thing on six legs (it can cover a metre in a second), and you really do have a recipe for real survival.

However, when it comes to durability, the cockroach has a rival.

The tardigrade.

Now, the tardigrade – great name, huh? – has a big advantage over the cockroach in that it's actually a microscopic creature. But, wow, what a creature! It can live for years without water in a dead, inert state with all its functions suspended, but then, with a little water, it can be brought back to life.

Technically the tardigrade is a *polyextremophile* and is able to survive in extreme conditions that would kill almost any other creature. It can survive temperatures as low as -272°C (close to absolute zero) and as high as 151°C.

It can also withstand 10 times more radiation than the cockroach.

So is there any doubt as to the winner of this particular contest?

Why do losers get 'booby prizes'?

Booby prizes – usually something really worthless and funny – are given to competitors who come last or get knocked out first.

There's a seabird called the booby which was thought to be particularly stupid. This was probably because it had a habit of landing on sailing ships, where it was easily captured and eaten.

So you can see why a stupid person might be called a booby – especially as the word itself *sounds* so silly!

From there, you can also see why a booby prize might be awarded to the person or team that comes bottom or last in any kind of contest.

Why do we describe someone who's talking nonsense as talking 'codswallop'? Does it have anything to do with the fish?

Possibly. There's a chance that the word derives from the sound – or wallop – that the offcuts from the cod made when falling to the ground in the filleting sheds.

However, I think it's much more likely that it comes from drink rather than from food. Specifically, beer. 'Wallop' is a slang word for beer. Even today, there are men who will talk about having a 'pint of wallop'.

In 1875 a man named Hiram Codd patented a bottle with a stopper for fizzy soft drinks. Beer-drinkers didn't like the sound of soft drinks but they *did* like the sound of Mr Codd's name.

So whenever they wanted to talk disparagingly about a soft drink – or, indeed, about a beer that was too weak (perhaps because it had been watered down) – they called it Codd's wallop.

In time, the word codswallop came to be used for anything that was rubbish or no good and, from there, for spoken rubbish or nonsense.

What was the first ever children's book?

First of all, let's exclude school books – on the basis that there would have been handwritten books for princes to use for studying.

The first ever children's book – printed in English – was a 1563 book of rhymes entitled *A Book in Englyshh Metre of the Great Merchant Man Called Dives Pragmaticus*. Consisting of just eight pages, it contained rhymes about Mr Dives Pragmaticus's business, and so not only was it the first children's book, it was also probably the first example of product placement in the media!

Are hot drinks more cooling than cold drinks when the weather's hot?

You'd think that a cold drink would cool you down, wouldn't you? Certainly, when it's hot, I find myself craving something cold in a glass full of ice.

However, this isn't necessarily a good idea. It might make you *think* you're cooling down but – apart from the rehydration your body obviously craves – it's doubtful whether it's actually doing anything to make you cooler.

And, indeed, there's the potential problem that if you drink a very cold drink too fast on a hot day, you might get stomach cramps.

In fact, when it comes to cooling down, it's not just a question of counteracting the outside air temperature (which is what a cold drink seems to do). What you're looking for is something to make you sweat and, if you like, match up your temperature inside and out.

A hot drink makes you sweat, which in turn takes heat away from your body and cools you down.

If you want further proof of this, then look at India, a country that experiences extremely high temperatures. There they drink cups of hot tea to keep cool. We'd be wise to follow their lead on this.

Why is it that even though black is most people's favourite fruit pastille, packets of all-black fruit pastilles are not as popular as the mixed packets?

I've probably thought longer and harder about this question than any other question in the book. All the surveys show that the most popular flavour for fruit pastilles – and fruit gums and wine gums, etc. – is blackcurrant (or blackberry).

I too love the black fruit pastilles (fruit gums/wine gums/hard gums) and, even as a supposedly wise old man, I've been known to grab as many as I can when I'm sharing a packet with my wife in the cinema (which is the only place I ever eat sweets!).

And yet, when I see a packet of all-black fruit pastilles, I never buy them.

Why?

It's crazy. I'm prefer them to all the other flavours – so why not eat them and only them?

And I'm not alone in this: other fans of black chewy sweets also reject the all-black packets in favour of the mixed ones.

After much contemplation – too much really, if I'm being honest and sensible – I've come to the conclusion that we need the other flavours to help us enjoy the black ones even more.

It's the same with boxes of chocolates: whatever your favourite centre, there's something rather wonderful about picking it out from all the other ones.

But this isn't just confined to sweets: lots of other things and activities are improved by blending them in with things that we don't enjoy quite as much. It's as though we thrive on the contrast as much as on the pleasure itself.

Take your favourite subject at school. Let's say it's English and that you look forward to

English classes. A whole day of English classes, on the other hand, might be boring: you need other subjects – even ones you don't like – to make the English lesson stand out.

What I'm saying is that anticipation – the act of wanting something, of looking forward to something – is a seriously important component of pleasure. If everything is equally enjoyable – even if it's really enjoyable – it eventually becomes dull.

This is why multi-millionaire rock stars are often so dissatisfied with life. If they've arranged for everything to be absolutely perfect, then not only do they howl with anguish whenever something goes even slightly wrong, they soon find that life is intolerable.

We need grit in our lives: that's the human condition. We have to strive for happiness and, yes, for perfection too. The journey is an important part of the process.

And that's why I buy mixed fruit pastilles instead of all-black ones.

Given that diamonds are the hardest substance known to man, how do they cut diamonds?

Fortunately, diamonds, like wood, have a grain and can be cut along the grain with a hard axe or against the grain with a special tool that has – wait for it! – a diamond edge.

Why do shops charge £19.99 instead of £20 (or £9.99 instead of £10, etc.)?

It's annoying, isn't it? And it doesn't fool us. If an item costs £4.99, we know we're not going to get too much change out of a fiver.

So why do shops do it?

There are two reasons for this practice, which is known as 'price rhetoric'.

The first is that, contrary to what you might think, there *are* people who are fooled/ reassured/enticed by a price tag that, at first glance, appears to be a whole pound cheaper (at the very least, they can reassure themselves that it's *less* than a certain amount).

However, the main reason why shops do it is that it forces staff to open the till and record the transaction rather than pocket the money handed over by the customer.

Take a book costing £5. If the customer hands over a £5 note, the shop assistant could, in theory, put that note straight in their pocket. However, if it's priced at £4.99, it's very unlikely that the customer will have the precise money, and so the shop assistant will be obliged to open the till and register the sale.

Of course, nowadays, almost every product has a barcode which has to be scanned, and besides, so many transactions are made with credit and debit cards. But still the practice continues: a 'tribute' to our gullibility and shop owners' lack of trust in their staff!

Why does Toblerone come in such an unusual shape?

Because the original makers took their inspiration from the Swiss mountain peaks which still feature on the cardboard packaging. It also meant that the bar was made up of convenient bite-sized pieces.

Toblerone was invented in Switzerland in 1908. It is probably the only chocolate 'shape' to have been patented, and the authorizing

signature was that of the scientific genius, Albert Einstein, who happened to be working in the Swiss Patent Office at the time.

The Tobler family had started making chocolate in 1867 in the town of Vevey, where the Nestlé family had also begun to produce their famous chocolates. Indeed, it was Nestlé who invented 'milk' chocolate by adding condensed milk to plain dark chocolate.

Jean Tobler died in 1905, leaving his company to his three children. Looking for a new product, they came across Montelimar

nougat – a mixture of almonds and pure honey. Jean, the son, and his cousin, Theodor Tobler, experimented combining nougat together with Tobler milk chocolate – in the kitchen rather than the factory. They called the resulting delicious concoction Toblerone, combining the family name with 'torrone', the Italian word for nougat.

Nowadays, Toblerone is the best-known Swiss chocolate in the world and is exported to more than 110 countries, and there's also a Mont Blanc version, containing white rather than brown chocolate.

Why are the headquarters of London's metropolitan police force known as Scotland Yard?

Quite! They should be known as London Yard or, at the very least, England Yard.

However, that would be to misunderstand the reason for the name.

The headquarters were originally located in a Whitehall street named Great Scotland Yard. This was so called because it was where Scottish kings – and their representatives – stayed when they came to London.

When the police needed larger premises, they moved to – yes, you've guessed it – headquarters they named New Scotland Yard.

How do they get the stripes into striped toothpaste?

This is a question I ask myself at least twice a day. It turns out to be quite simple.

The tube is filled to a certain level with white toothpaste. Above that level, it is filled with the 'stripy' stuff, which is usually red, blue or green. Both materials are viscous enough so that they don't mix. When you squeeze the tube, you let these two substances out at the same time.

Here, you must understand that the toothpaste nozzle isn't just a hole at the top of the tube. Instead, it's a longish straw that reaches down the tube to the top of the (white) toothpaste. The straw (or pipe) has small holes in it closer to the nozzle. Pressing the tube causes the white stuff to enter the outlet pipe and trigger the stripy stuff, which now enters the outlet pipe through the small holes – which is where the stripes are generated.

Was there a real Goody Two-Shoes?

Goody Two-Shoes was a character in an 18th-century fairy tale.

In the original story, which has echoes of *Cinderella*, Goody Two-Shoes was a poor orphan named Margery Meanwell who was so poor, she only had one shoe. However, a rich benefactor gave her a pair of shoes. She was so happy – yeah, I know, easily pleased – that she went around telling everyone about her 'two shoes'.

Eventually Margery married a rich man and – well, you can guess the rest, but you can be pretty sure that there was quite a lot of living happily ever after.

Evidently they liked that kind of thing in those days. *These days* we're a lot more cynical, and so the name Goody Two-Shoes isn't used as a compliment but almost as a term of abuse for someone who wears their virtue – or goodness – on their sleeve.

Why do dogs overheat in parked cars?

This has everything to do with selfish owners and dogs' inability to sweat effectively.

The average body temperature for a dog is 38.4 degrees Celsius. This is actually higher than our average body temperature of 37 degrees, so theoretically they should be able to take hotter conditions than we can.

However, dogs don't have sweat glands except in their paws, so the only way they can lose heat is by panting. In a matter of minutes the interior of a car parked in the sun on a hot summer's day can become unbearably hot – well above the dog's body temperature. Even on a relatively cool day, the temperature inside a parked car can rise to life-threatening levels if the sun is out. In fact, researchers at the Stanford University School of Medicine found that there had been cases of dogs dying in temperatures as low as 21 degrees Celsius.

Leaving a car window open might help a

little – leaving two open and allowing a cross-breeze slightly more – but not much. So, unless it's for literally just a couple of minutes, dogs should NOT be left in parked cars.

Why is someone who's facing humiliation said to be eating humble pie? Is there such a dish?

There is – or, at least, there *was*. In the 14th century 'numble' was the name given to the heart, liver, lungs, entrails, etc., of animals (especially deer). 'Numble' came from the French word *nomble*, meaning a deer's innards. Later, the word 'numble' became 'umble'. When the lord and his family ate venison or some other meat, the umble (or umbles) was put into a pie and sent down the end of the table for the servants to eat.

Meanwhile, the word 'humble' means modest

or inferior, and although it has nothing whatsoever to do with the umble pie, you can see why the two would have become confused – especially as many people drop the 'h' in speech (making humble and umble sound exactly the same).

And that's just what happened. As the dish itself disappeared from our lives, the expression itself remained – as humble (rather than umble) pie.

So you'd have to be pretty humble to eat humble pie, and after eating it, you'd feel even humbler!

Why are we said to 'pass the buck' when we're avoiding responsibility?

Your teacher asks you to show some new children around the school. You don't want to do this and so you persuade your friend to do it instead. 'No,' says the teacher on finding out what you have arranged, 'you have to do it: you can't pass the buck.'

So what is this buck that gets passed around (or not)?

It actually comes from the game of poker. The card game – often played for high stakes – became very popular in the US in the 19th century. Players were understandably suspicious of cheats, and since the dealer has the best opportunity to cheat, it became the practice for the deal to change with each hand. To work out whose turn it was to deal, a marker was placed in front of the dealer, and this would be passed clockwise after each hand of cards.

Nowadays, this marker is a small round disc with the word DEALER on it. But in 19th–century America, the marker was usually a knife, and because knives often had handles made of buck's horn, the marker became known as a buck.

When the dealer's turn was done, he 'passed the buck'. In other words, he was handing over the responsibility for dealing – an activity which, in the Wild West, was very risky.

Soon the expression spread outside the world of gambling into general speech. It became especially popular during the presidency of Harry Truman (1945–53), who had a sign in his office bearing the words: THE BUCK STOPS HERE. In other words, there was no one to whom he, as President of the United States, could pass the buck: he *had* to take responsibility.

Why does sand come in different colours?

It's true that sand comes in different colours. It can vary from white to yellow to black. And yet it's still the same basic substance: sand.

That's because all types of sand are created from the weathering and erosion of rock or minerals, and these vary enormously. So in Lanzarote (in the Canary Islands) the sand is formed from the erosion of volcanic deposits and so it's black; whereas in the Caribbean they have fine white sands formed as a result of the erosion of coral.

Same principle; different substances – which explains the different colours.

Are there really just six degrees of separation between human beings?

That's probably about right. That's to say, there are just six people who link you with any other person in the world.

OK, let's exclude people in really remote parts of the globe – like the Amazonian rainforests or Papua New Guinea – but it's surprising just how easily we all link up.

The idea of six degrees of separation, by which someone can be connected to anyone else in just six steps, emerged from the experiments of Stanley Milgram at Harvard University in the 1960s. Milgram sent packages to 160 random

people from the state of Nebraska and asked them to forward their package to someone who would be better placed to get it to the target recipient, a Boston stockbroker. The majority, Milgram claimed, made it to Boston within six steps.

The phrase was popularized by the Broadway play, *Six Degrees of Separation* by John Guare, inspired by the life of a conman called David Hampton, who posed as the actor Sidney Poitier's son and swindled many New York celebrities out of thousands of dollars.

Is there any harm in filling the kettle from the hot tap?

In fact, might it not be better than using the cold tap? After all, it would take less time – and therefore use up less energy – to boil a kettle of hot (rather than cold) water.

However – and it's a big however – there is a massive drawback to using the hot tap. The tank that holds the (cold) drinking water in your home is properly covered and so the water that comes out of the cold tap is clean and suitable

for drinking. The tank that feeds the hot-water system in most homes is usually a lot less secure and – *are-you-sure-you-want-to-read-this alert!* – often has dead birds, rodents and insects in it.

So if you were to fill the kettle from the hot tap – and my advice is: DON'T – then you'd have to make sure you boiled the kettle for an awfully long time (at least four minutes) just to make sure you killed all the bacteria. The extra time would therefore almost certainly exceed the time you'd have saved from using hot water in the first place.

Oh, and boiled cold water contains more oxygen than boiled warm water, and that makes hot drinks taste better (apparently).

Was there a Mary who had a little lamb?

Yes there was! You must remember the old nursery rhyme:

Mary had a little lamb
Whose fleece was white as snow,
And everywhere that Mary went,
The lamb was sure to go.

It followed her to school one day,
Which was against the rule.
It made the children laugh and play
To see a lamb at school.

And so the teacher turned it out,
But still it lingered near,
And waited patiently about
Till Mary did appear.

This nursery rhyme goes back to the year 1830 and was inspired by something that actually happened.

A girl named Mary Sawyer kept a pet lamb which, egged on by her brother, she took

to school – with the consequences that are described in the nursery rhyme.

There's some doubt as to who wrote the rhyme. It might have been a poet named Sarah Josepha Hale (who certainly published it) or it might have been a young divinity student named John Roulstone, who actually witnessed the lamb incident.

Mary Sawyer herself believed that it was Roulstone, but it's entirely possible that he just wrote the first verse and showed Ms Hale, who then wrote the rest of it.

In any event, it happened!

A couple of years later, it was set to music and became a proper nursery rhyme rather than just a poem.

How was grass cut before the invention of the lawnmower?

The first thing to say is that until the lawnmower was invented (in 1830), people didn't really have lawns or, indeed, gardens. It was the very invention of the lawnmower that prompted people to start having lawns in the first place! Before then, for most ordinary people, land wasn't for gardens (as we understand them) but a place to grow vegetables and herbs or to graze livestock. Of course, the grazing itself kept the grass short, but that was a by-product rather than the intention.

The only people who bothered to have proper lawns were – surprise, surprise – the very wealthy. Their lawns were kept in peak condition by the use of a scythe – a sharp round-bladed tool. Obviously, this required many man-hours, but labour costs were very low and so that didn't bother the landowners very much.

Incidentally, if you don't have a lawnmower and you have to keep the grass down, you could do a lot worse than use rabbits and chickens. They'll produce a neat and short lawn, but the best possible natural 'lawnmower' is the guinea pig, which never stops eating – and even likes the weeds.

What's the best thing to do if you fall into quicksand?

Don't panic!

Nothing bad is going to happen to you . . . unless you panic. In that sense, falling into quicksand is no different from suddenly finding yourself out of your depth in the sea.

Quicksand is a solution of salt water, sand and clay. Although it appears to be solid, the tiniest pressure is enough to set off a chain reaction, separating the water and sand particles. That's what starts the sinking process.

Here's the bad news: quicksand is sticky –
very sticky. To remove your foot at a speed of
1cm/sec requires the same force needed to
lift a car.

However – and here's the good news – there
is little chance of sinking more than waist
deep in the stuff. And, if you don't panic,
you will NOT drown. In fact, you can't sink
in quicksand if you lie on your back as it's
heavier than water and you can't help but
float in it.

But, hey, best keep away from it altogether,
don't you think?

Why are slugs so slimy?

Slugs thrive in the wet. If they dry out – a process known as *desiccation* – they die. So they have to produce a protective mucus – which looks like slime to us – to survive.

Of course, when it's raining they're fine, and that is why most of them are really active after rain. When it's dry, they hide in damp places – under tree bark, fallen logs, rocks and flower pots – so they stay damp, and survive. If that doesn't do the trick, it's slime time.

This nasty-tasting stuff also provides protection against predators as it makes the slug hard to pick up and hold – for example in a bird's beak. Given that slugs have so many predators – frogs, toads, hedgehogs, snakes, birds, etc. – they need all the help they can get. Slugs also have the ability to contract their bodies to make themselves harder and more compact, and so even more difficult for predators to grab.

But slime doesn't just protect slugs from

predators, it also helps them when they're moving around. The slime contains fibres which help them to grip when they're going up and down vertical surfaces.

But that's not all! The 'slime trail' that slugs leave behind allows other slugs to recognize possible mates.

Clever little things, slugs – but they don't make the most cuddly of pets!

What can you do in just two minutes?

Hmm, that's not very long, is it? But, in fact, it's just long enough to . . .

Fly the 1.5 miles between the Orcadian islands of Westray and Papa Westray – at just two minutes, it's the world's shortest scheduled flight.

Scramble an egg: you don't have time to boil one.

Rap 1,464 syllables, if you're world's fastest rapper, Rebel XD.

Run two minutes of advertising on a top-rated US TV show . . . for $2.3 million.

Eat 56 frankfurters at world-record speed.

Wash them down with 24 yards of ale.

Have 17 bananas for pudding.

Boil a pint of water in an average domestic kettle.

Watch TV and burn off 2.4 calories.

Yodel 2,640 tones at world-record pace.

Cover 4.2611 metres if you're a three-toed sloth.

Cover two miles if you're a cheetah.

Travel 22.32 million miles at the speed of light.

Dance the salsa,
swim or run: your
choice for 25 calories.

Listen to The Beatles'
All My Loving, which
lasts *precisely* two
minutes.

Ride the Pepsi Max Big One
roller-coaster on Blackpool's
Pleasure Beach (it takes
precisely two minutes).

Travel 13 miles in the world
record-breaking Thrust SSC
rocket car.

Travel 25.3 miles at the speed of
sound.

Swim 0.000033 miles if you're a
seahorse.

Have your tyres changed and petrol
tank filled about 15 times if you're an
Formula One driver.

Experience 0.13 per cent of a mayfly's
lifespan.

Why, when people are happy, are they said to be 'tickled pink'?

Yes – why not tickled blue or tickled orange? Why *pink*?

For a very simple reason: when people get really excited, their skin becomes flushed – turning a shade of pink (just like when we blush). Technically, what happens is that our blood vessels dilate, more blood flows close to the skin, and we turn slightly pinker.

What is pot luck?

Nowadays, you're as likely to see 'pot luck' as a category in a quiz – where it means 'questions on any subject' – as anywhere else.

This isn't too far from its original meaning of taking your chance on what you might be given to eat.

Perhaps you've heard someone inviting a guest over for supper at the last minute, saying, 'I don't know what we've got – will you take pot luck?' In other words, Will you take whatever we happen to have?

So that's the 'luck' part of pot luck explained . . . what about the pot?

This goes back to the practice – in poorer times than ours – of never throwing away any leftovers, but putting them in a pot on the stove to keep warm. This pot could then be used to feed people at short notice – especially in taverns and inns in medieval times, where you turned up and took the 'luck of the pot'. A similar idea exists in

France, where an unplanned meal is often referred to as *pot au feu* – literally 'pot on the fire'.

What exactly is haggis?

Haggis is a traditional Scottish dish which is always served – with much ceremony – on Burns Night (25 January, which is the birthday of the poet Robert Burns).

This brings to mind the clerihew:

One often yearns
For the land of Burns;
The only snag is
The haggis.

Well, I'm not sure you'll disagree with me when you hear what's in it.

There are many different recipes, but typically it will include a sheep's innards (heart, liver and lungs), minced and mixed with onion, oatmeal, suet, spices and salt. As if that isn't gruesome enough, traditionally it's cooked in an animal's stomach – although these days it's often prepared in the sort of casing they use for sausages.

At least the traditional accompaniments aren't so grisly. It's usually served with 'neeps and tatties' (turnips and potatoes) and a glass of Scotch whisky.

Why do people say 'as sure is eggs is eggs'?

They do, you know, when they're trying to get across the idea that something is absolutely certain to happen.

For example, 'If my football team doesn't spend more money on players, then, as sure as eggs is eggs, we'll be relegated.'

But why eggs? What's so 'sure' about them?

All becomes clear when you realize that the expression should really be 'as sure as *x* is *x*' – which is a logician or mathematician's formula.

After all, what could be more certain – especially to a mathematician – than the fact that *x* equals *x*?

Why does = equal equals?

The equals sign (=) in mathematics was invented or introduced by Robert Recorde

in 1557. Mr Recorde, a Welsh physician and mathematician, decided on the symbol on the basis that nothing was more equal than two parallel lines.

And who can disagree?

For the record – excuse the pun – poor Mr Recorde died in prison the following year.

Which didn't 'equal' a very good result . . .

woof!
woof!

Why do we talk about someone 'barking up the wrong tree' when they're making a mistake?

This comes from raccoon hunting. Dogs were used to hunt raccoons by following their scent. When they found one taking refuge up a tree, they would stop at the bottom and bark. However, because raccoons are nocturnal, hunting took place in the dark, and sometimes the dogs would – you guessed it! – bark at the bottom of the wrong tree.

What's the most humiliating thing that's ever happened to anyone?

That's a tough call. I myself have had plenty of humiliating moments – not least just the other day when I attempted to wipe (what I thought was) a breadcrumb off a friend's face, only to discover that it was, in fact, a spot. Oops!

But for real *public* humiliation, you can't get much worse than the 1933 Academy Awards ceremony. Frank Capra was so certain he would win the Best Director Oscar for *Lady for a Day* that he began to rise before Will Rogers had even finished announcing the winner. Capra made his way up to the stage as Rogers said: 'Come on up and get it, Frank.'

But the winner turned out to be another Frank – Frank Lloyd for *Cavalcade*. Capra called his return to his seat 'the longest, saddest, most shattering walk in my life'.

I hope the worst thing that's ever happened to you in public is a lot less embarrassing than that!

Why are people said to be 'climbing on the bandwagon' when they support a popular person or cause?

This started in the US, where salesmen used a band of musicians to play on the back of a truck or wagon to draw a crowd. So it became known as a bandwagon. During elections, political candidates would use musicians in the same way – effectively urging people to climb on the bandwagon.

Why is someone who's always in a bad mood said to have 'a chip on their shoulder'?

This dates back to the US of the early 19th century, when bars had sawdust floors. A man who felt like picking a fight would pick up a wood chip from the floor and place it on his shoulder, challenging someone – anyone – to knock it off.

He therefore had a chip on his shoulder which, with all the alcohol being drunk, would almost certainly be knocked off by one or more of his fellow drinkers!

Why does our skin go wrinkly when we've stayed in the bath for too long?

The outer layer of your skin (the epidermis) produces an oily substance called sebum, which you can see when you touch a window, a mirror or some other shiny surface: it's the oily mark you leave there.

Normally, this sebum keeps water off your skin. However, when you go into the water – the bath, the sea, swimming pools – the sebum gets washed off and your skin starts to absorb water.

The skin on your hands (especially the palms) and your feet (especially the soles) is thicker than anywhere else, and so it's there that all this water-absorbing is most obvious – creating the wrinkles that you notice.

Thankfully, when you get out of the bath and dry off, the water evaporates and your skin shrinks back to the same size as the tissue underneath. So you won't be permanently wrinkly – phew!

Was there ever a Little Tommy Tucker who sang for his supper?

Little Tommy Tucker
Sings for his supper.
What shall we give him?
White bread and butter.
How shall he cut it
Without a knife?
How will he be married
Without a wife?

This 19th-century nursery rhyme is about

orphans – boys and girls without mothers
or fathers. In the 18th century, an orphan
was often called 'Little Tommy Tucker' and
orphans were indeed often reduced to
begging – or singing – for their supper. And,
as orphans, they wouldn't have had knives
to cut their bread and butter. Given such
poverty, it would be impossible for a (male)
orphan to provide for a wife.

Why do the Americans call the last letter of the alphabet 'zee' when we call it 'zed'?

As regular readers will know, when it comes to matters of pronunciation, I'm perfectly prepared to put my hands up and say that the Americans are right and that we Brits are wrong.

In fact, though, in this instance, we're right and the Yanks are wrong.

Why, I hear you ask, is that? Surely, if the letters B, C, D, G, P, T and V are all pronounced 'bee', 'see', 'dee', 'gee', 'pee', 'tee' and 'vee' (rather than 'bed', 'sed', 'ded', 'ged', 'ped', 'ted' and 'ved'), then why shouldn't the letter Z be pronounced 'zee' rather than 'zed'?

Fair point, but those aren't the only letters in the alphabet: just one group, if you like, and it so happens that Z (like more than half the others) isn't one of them.

To explain why, we have to go back to the origins of our language.

We get the last letter of our alphabet from the French, where the equivalent is pronounced as 'zed'. Incidentally, it is pronounced the same way in German.

Meanwhile, the Italians and the Spanish call it 'zeta'. This comes from the Latin which, in turn, came from the Greek. But how did the ancient Greeks pronounce their Ts? As Ds!

I rest my case!

The fact is that the Americans changed a lot of things after they won independence from us, and that included some pronunciations.

In other cases (e.g. the pronunciation of the word 'lieutenant'), it was we who changed and they who stayed on the true path.

Here, though, they changed it and, not to put too fine a point on it, got it wrong.

Alas, with the popularity of American films and television, many non-Americans – including our fellow countrymen – now pronounce Z as 'zee'. It's up to all of us to put them right when they do it (unless, of course, they're a lot bigger and stronger!).

Is the kiwi fruit named after the kiwi bird?

The kiwi fruit originally came from China, and it was first known as the Chinese gooseberry because people thought it was small and prickly like a traditional gooseberry.

But in New Zealand it was recultivated to be larger and fleshier and sweeter, and so the

New Zealanders renamed it the kiwi fruit to differentiate it from the smaller original fruit.

The kiwi is the national bird of New Zealand and also the country's emblem. So naming it the kiwi fruit was an obvious attempt to link it to the country itself.

Apart from that, there's no connection between the bird and the fruit: the bird doesn't even eat the fruit.

Very few people – even New Zealanders (or Kiwis, as they confusingly call themselves!) – have actually seen a kiwi in the wild. I've seen one – but only in the dark in a special sanctuary, as they're shy, nocturnal creatures.

The kiwi is the sole survivor of an ancient order of birds. It's never had any predators so it never needed to fly and its tiny little wings are useless. However, despite its awkward appearance, a kiwi can actually outrun a human; it's managed to survive because of its speed and alertness and sharp, three-toed feet, which enable it to kick and slash an enemy. It has an excellent sense of smell and feeds on worms, insects and grubs, but not – repeat not! – the kiwi fruit.

Why is Kent known as the garden of England?

Yes indeed! I can understand that the garden would be at the back – or bottom – of the country, but why not Surrey, Dorset, Hampshire, Devon, Essex, Wiltshire or (my own dear county) Sussex?

Why Kent?

Kent earned the title because of all its orchards, hop gardens and market gardens (where they grow the fruit and vegetables that feed the capital). Kent also has one other feature that makes it a garden: it's one of the warmest parts of the country. On 10 August 2003 the Kent town of Brogdale recorded a temperature of 38.5 degrees Celsius, which is the hottest ever recorded in the United Kingdom.

However, there are other counties which have threatened to wrestle the title from Kent. Worcestershire, which has a lot of apple orchards, has also been called the Garden

of England, while North Yorkshire beat both Worcestershire and Kent in a BBC TV viewers' poll to judge the county with the best gardens.

But Kent is still the answer to the question 'Which county is the garden of England?'!

Are there loos in igloos?

Well, it's a thought, isn't it? And it certainly makes a fun title for the book, so let me try to answer it.

Firstly, these days Eskimos – or *Inuits*, as they are now known – no longer live in igloos (or 'iglus', as they are now known). They live in flats and houses like you and me – well, me anyway: for all I know, you live in a tepee or a castle or, indeed, an igloo. Sorry, *iglu* . . .

But obviously people used to live in igloos, so the question is still relevant – even if only to satisfy historical curiosity.

The answer is that they DID have loos in

igloos – well, it beat having to venture out into the cold where, presumably, their pee would ice up in the very act of peeing. And then there were the polar bears: you wouldn't want to encounter one of them while you were answering the call of nature. However, the igloos were made up of more

than just a single snow room. They'd make a big igloo and then they'd add on extra igloos for storage and also for a toilet. How they disposed of their waste from the toilet would have depended on circumstances, but would have involved digging holes and covering them with copious amounts of snow.

Was there a 'Little Boy Blue' – as in the nursery rhyme?

Do you know the nursery rhyme in question? This is how it goes:

Little Boy Blue,
Come blow your horn.
The sheep's in the meadow,
The cow's in the corn;

Where is that boy
Who looks after the sheep?
Under the haystack
Fast asleep.

Will you wake him?
Oh no, not I,
For if I do
He will surely cry.

It's thought that 'Little Boy Blue' refers to Cardinal Thomas Wolsey (1475–1530), who was King Henry VIII's right-hand man. Wolsey was a wealthy, arrogant man with lots of enemies. Having got his university degree at the age of 15, he was dubbed the 'Boy

Bachelor'. As the owner of Hampton Court Palace, he was also just the sort of boaster who might 'blow his own horn'. But Wolsey wasn't born into wealth: he was the son of a butcher, and it's entirely possible that he might have looked after the sheep in his youth – something his enemies would have really enjoyed pointing out.

Why do leaves change colour in the autumn?

They don't!

To which you might reply: *Are you sure? They're green in summer and yellow in autumn – that looks like a change to me.*

That's as maybe, but they don't actually change colour. What happens is this. They normally look green because they contain chlorophyll. When the leaf dies, the chlorophyll disappears and the other colours – especially the yellow – that were there all along, emerge.

Why can't we drink seawater?

Although we all need to consume a certain amount of salt – about 500mg a day – just to remain alive, excess consumption is dangerous and potentially fatal.

Put it this way. Salt makes up only 0.25 per cent of our total body weight (though the salt content of our blood is about 0.9 per

cent). Seawater is over 3 per cent dissolved salt – which is at least three times more than we can tolerate. So although you might physically be able to swallow seawater (and I would strongly advise against it), your body – and especially your kidneys – wouldn't be able to tolerate it.

Which is why you'd almost certainly throw up within seconds of drinking it.

However, let's suppose that you were lost at sea in a dinghy with no fresh water and you were dying of thirst. Would it be worth drinking seawater in the absence of any other fluid?

The answer is no. In fact, the seawater would leave you even thirstier as all the fluid in your body attempted to dilute the sudden intake of salt. In other words, the salted water wouldn't hydrate you but *dehydrate* you. The more you drank, the thirstier you'd get.

How cruel is that?

In other words, once you started drinking seawater – especially in such desperate circumstances – you'd get so thirsty that you'd feel the need to drink more and more of it until you suffered permanent brain damage. But before that occurred, the salt water would work its way to your kidneys, which would be overwhelmed and shut down. You can't live without functioning kidneys and so you would die.

So my advice to you is twofold: never drink seawater and, if you're going to sea in a small boat, take lots of fresh water with you.

Has the foxglove flower anything to do with foxes?

Despite its name, it hasn't. In fact, it's a corruption of 'folks' gloves', as fairies were said to use flowers as gloves. The Latin name for the foxglove – *Digitalis* – refers to the flowers' finger- or digit-like shape. Foxgloves are poisonous to eat (my wife's chicken once ate one and fell off its perch that very night – stone dead).

Talking of poisonous plants, when potatoes were first introduced to Britain, a lot of people refused to eat them because the leaves of the potato plant look very similar to the leaves of deadly nightshade, which are of course poisonous.

Why do people say 'Hear! Hear!' when they agree with something that someone has said?

This comes from public meetings when someone would get up and speak – only to be interrupted by other people. Those supporting the speaker would shout 'Hear him!' which, eventually, became 'Hear! Hear!'

Why is it that when we go to sleep we go to the Land of Nod?

For the answer to this question we have to go all the way back to the very first chapter of the Bible. After Cain murdered his brother Abel, he fled to the Land of Nod.

And Cain went out from the presence of the LORD, and dwelt in the land of Nod, on the east of Eden. (Genesis 4:16)

The Hebrew word *nod* means 'wandering'.

How entering the Land of Nod came to mean falling asleep isn't clear – beyond the thought that you sort of 'wander off' to sleep. And of course we 'nod off' when we go to sleep. It isn't hard to see the connection between 'nodding off' and the Land of Nod, is it?

Why is the leek associated with Wales?

Proudly sported every St David's Day (1 March), the leek is now widely recognized as the national symbol of Wales.

This tradition goes back to at least the 15th century. During Elizabethan times, Shakespeare refers to the custom of wearing a leek as an 'ancient tradition', and his character Henry V tells Fluellen that he is wearing a leek, 'for I am Welsh, you know, good countryman'.

Also, entries in the household accounts of the (Welsh) Tudor kings of England record payments

for leeks worn by the household guards on St David's Day.

It's hard to know where this tradition started, but it might have been when, in the seventh century, King Cadwaladr of Gwynedd told his soldiers to identify themselves in a battle against the Saxons by wearing leeks on their helmets (the battle took place in a leek field).

Many Welsh people have substituted the daffodil for the leek, perhaps because it looks more attractive and certainly smells a lot better. Interesting to note, however, that one of the many Welsh names for a daffodil is *Cenhinen Bedr*, or 'Peter's leek'.

What happened in Britain between 3 and 14 September 1752?

Absolutely nothing!

Come off it, *something* must have happened – even if it was only boring stuff that no one bothered to record?

Nope, nothing happened whatsoever. Why? Well, you might have guessed by now that this is a trick question (and one well worth trying out on your teachers or family!). Nothing happened because these dates never existed.

Let me explain.

In 1752 Britain (and its empire) switched from the Julian calendar to the Gregorian calendar. In order to make it happen, we had to adjust our date to the same date as all the other countries using the Gregorian calendar. The easiest way to do that was to simply cancel the dates between 3 and 14 September.

The British public didn't like this adjustment: in fact, people rioted for the return of their 11 days. It must have been particularly awful for people whose birthdays fell in those lost days!

What makes a gooseberry fool dessert so foolish?

It's not foolish – it's just that the fool in gooseberry fool (or any other fruit fool) comes from the French word *fouler*, meaning to crush. Which is, after all, what happens to the fruit in a fruit fool.

Why do people put 'NB' after they've written something?

NB means 'note well' and it comes from the initials of the Latin words *nota bene*, which mean just that. It's merely a way of adding something – to a letter (though there you'd usually put PS for 'post script') or article or essay – that helps to illuminate a thought or point.

Is a lido so called because it's a place where you can lie down?

Well, that's what I always thought! But no, it turns out that it isn't. Lidos are public outdoor swimming pools (with surrounding facilities), or part of a beach where people can swim and lie in the sun. So it makes sense that it would be derived from the words 'lie down'.

Instead, the word comes from the Lido – the sandy barrier beach that encloses the lagoon of Venice, where sea-bathing took place from the late 19th century onwards.

What was the first novel ever written?

It is generally agreed that the world's first novel was *The Tale of Genji*. It was written by the Japanese noblewoman Murasaki Shikibu (or Lady Murasaki – although both of these were pseudonyms) in or around AD 1007.

To whom was the very first passport issued?

That's hard to say for sure, but passports have been around in some form or other for thousands of years. The first recorded passport goes back to 445 BC, when the

prophet Nehemiah wanted to travel from Persia to his home in Judah. He asked the Persian King Artaxerxes to give him a letter for 'the governors of the country beyond the river', requesting safe passage.

Well, that's a passport in anyone's language.

The Romans too saw the need for travellers to be identified as Roman citizens – with all the protection that entailed – when going abroad. So Romans were given documents – effectively passports – that helped them in foreign lands and allowed them to return to Rome.

Since then, 'letters of transit' and similar documents have been used by diplomats and travellers. British passports were first mentioned during the reign of Henry V in 1414. Known as 'Safe Conducts', they were bits of paper personally signed by the king or queen, asking for the bearer to travel freely. In later centuries, British passports were individually printed and signed by the Secretary of State. Between 1772 and 1858 British passports were written in French. There were very few issued because so few

people travelled overseas. To have a British passport at that time you had to know the Foreign Secretary personally or know someone who knew him so that it could be signed by him. It was also very expensive. A passport cost over £2, at a time when the annual wage of a housemaid was £12. But then, of course, housemaids didn't go abroad.

The use of passports by all countries is a 20th-century development and it came about because of the First World War and worries over security. It was at this time that photographs were added to passports – an idea that developed from the 19th-century French fashion for fixing photographs to visiting cards.

From 1915 the passport was a single page folded into eight. It had a photograph, a signature and a thorough personal description of its holder, including features (e.g. eyes: large, nose: small), shape of face (e.g. round) and complexion (e.g. tanned).

Does *supercalifragilisticexpialidocious* actually mean anything?

We all know the word – even if some of us can't pronounce it properly – from the film *Mary Poppins*. But presumably it was just a silly – if wonderful – word made up specifically for the film?

Well, that's what I thought until I took a closer look . . .

When the film came out in 1964, the song 'Supercalifragilisticexpialidocious' was an instant hit . . . with everyone except a couple of songwriters who'd written a song called 'Supercalafajaistickespeealadojus' 15 years earlier and had actually shown it to Disney (the film's producers). They – not unreasonably – brought a legal case against the composers of 'Supercalifragilisticexpialidocious' for several million dollars. However, they lost because, after listening to several witnesses, the judge

decided that the word – or words like it – had been in use for years before either song was written.

No one had any idea what the word meant – if anything – with the composers of the *Mary Poppins* song claiming that it was just 'a very long word that had been passed down in many variations through many generations of kids'. The word was first coined in 1918, and was supposed to be even harder to say than 'antidisestablishmentarianism'.

So there you have it: just a long meaningless word, but it has brought pleasure to millions!

Has anyone ever really *seen* a ghost?

When it comes to ghosts – and, indeed, any example of the paranormal – I am a total sceptic.

Fortunately, I'm not alone. In 2003 university psychologists, with the aid of 900 volunteers, 'proved' once and for all that there are no such things as ghosts.

So why do people think there are?

The reason why people 'believe' in ghosts, ghouls, poltergeists, etc., is because they choose to. Apart from anything else, it's more exciting than the alternative and makes the ghost-spotter sound jolly interesting when they tell their friends afterwards.

At this point, let me introduce you to something called 'Occam's Razor', which basically states: 'The simplest explanation for a phenomenon is most likely the correct explanation.' In other words, if you see an 'apparition' and you're not sure whether it's

a ghost or your brother/sister/friend winding you up, go for the option that's the most likely (clue: not a ghost).

Having said that, I can tell you that, apparently, we reach the peak of our ability to see ghosts at the age of seven; that 12 per cent of Britons believe they have seen ghosts; and that an astonishing 68 per cent of Britons say they believe in the existence of ghosts and/or spirits.

Meanwhile, I should also – in the spirit (no pun intended) of open-mindedness – list famous people who say that they have seen ghosts:

The Queen: When they were children, the Queen and her sister, Princess Margaret, reckon that they saw the ghost of Queen Elizabeth I at Windsor Castle.

Daniel Day-Lewis: When he was acting in _Hamlet_ in 1989, the Oscar-winning star thought he saw the ghost of his father (the late Poet Laureate Cecil Day-Lewis). After the actor playing the ghost of Hamlet's father said, 'I am thy father's spirit,' Daniel Day-Lewis went off stage and wouldn't come back

– convinced that he'd 'seen' his father.

Sting: The rock star awoke to 'find' a 'figure' dressed in Victorian clothes. He thought it was his wife but she was in bed next to him. She also saw this apparition and they held each other tight, staring at it until it simply faded away, never to return.

June Brown: The actress who found fame as Dot Cotton in *EastEnders* saw something worse than a ghost: she saw a ghostly tunnel. She was walking with a friend along an abandoned single-track railway line and saw a tunnel, which they started to walk down. Realizing that the tunnel had no end and feeling a little spooked, they turned and ran back. The next day they went back to where they had entered the tunnel and found that it had mysteriously vanished.

Prince Charles: Some years ago, he and his then valet, Ken Stronach, entered the library at Sandringham. Suddenly they felt inexplicably cold and became convinced that someone was standing behind them, but when they looked round, there was no one there. Understandably, they ran out.

Will Young: The singer claims that he saw a ghost while staying in a converted monastery in the south of France.

Kerry Katona: The one-time singer and TV personality says her house is haunted by a ghost that blows up light bulbs.

I'm not doubting the sincerity of any of the

above – heaven forfend! – but I still don't believe in ghosts, etc., and, to cap it all, I'll leave with you this thought. Isn't it strange that, with so many people having mobile phones that take photographs and video clips, there's never been a scientifically authenticated image.

I rest my case.

Is there a name for the hollow bit of the ear leading to the eardrum?

Yes, there is, and it's called the *alveary*. It's an interesting word that also means 'beehive' or, in Latin, several beehives. And why is it called that? Because anatomists thought that the shape of the eardrum resembled that of a beehive.

Is it true that it's illegal to dress up as Batman in Australia?

No, don't be silly! And yet there are people who will tell you that it is. Which is why I thought I'd nail this myth once and for all. This claim came about because of an obscure law which prohibits the wearing of dark clothes all over the body for fear that people

will look like cat burglars. Given that the Batman costume is pretty much all black, some people insist that it is covered by this law and that therefore it must be illegal to dress up as Batman.

Fortunately for Batman fans who want to dress up as their hero, the law *doesn't* include them. Besides, it would be a pretty stupid cat burglar who'd dress up as the caped crusader. After all, it's hardly the best way of avoiding attention!

Why do we give – and receive – Easter eggs?

The giving of eggs at Easter started when eggs were forbidden by the Church during Lent. As this coincided with peak laying time, there were large surpluses, and so the custom developed of hand-painting them and swapping them as gifts or keepsakes.

Even in pre-Christian times, the egg was always a symbol of new life and, as with so many pagan symbols and rituals, this transferred neatly into Christian practices.

Lent, the 40 days leading up to Easter, is traditionally a time when people forsake favourite foods and drink. Many people do without chocolate, so you can see why, in the 19th century, people decided that combining chocolate and eggs to make chocolate Easter eggs would be a jolly good idea.

Why is it that when you drop a piece of toast, it always lands buttered side down?

It doesn't. You just remember the occasions when it does because it's so annoying. Also, our brains hate randomness: we always look for patterns. It is unsatisfactory to think that the side on which the toast falls is down to chance: how much more reassuring to think that there's a scientific basis to it – even if it's only Murphy's Law: Anything that *can* go wrong *will* go wrong.

In fact, there have been some serious studies to discover if toast does indeed usually fall buttered side down and, if so, why?

I won't bore you with the physics (not least

because I don't fully understand it), but basically those scientists who reckon that it does fall buttered side down say that it's because it starts from a position of buttered side up and does a 180-degree flip to buttered side down on its fall to the ground. Believe it or not, these scientists will have actually spent several hours dropping bits of toast – in laboratory conditions, naturally – just to see how they landed.

Lucky there's nothing more serious to study . . .

Actually, the best riposte to these scientists is to cite Finagle's First Three Laws (all responses to Murphy's Law):

Finagle's First Law: If an experiment works, something has gone wrong.

Finagle's Second Law: No matter what the experiment's result, there will always be someone eager to: a) misinterpret it; b) fake it; or c) believe it supports his own pet theory.

Finagle's Third Law: In any collection of data, the figure most obviously correct, beyond all need of checking, is the mistake.

How do they measure the distance between cities?

I've often wondered about that. When you're in a car and you see a sign for, say, Chester that says CHESTER 21 MILES – what does it mean? Is it 21 miles to the outskirts of that city, to the centre or to the furthest point?

In fact, the distances between cities are actually the distances between city halls. So when you see the sign that says CHESTER 21 MILES, it means you're 21 miles from Chester's city hall.

It's as good a system as any.

Why are there 13 in a baker's dozen?

As you know, there are 12 in a dozen: no more, no less. However, there are 13 in a baker's dozen. Why?

In the 13th century there was a law called the Assize of Bread and Ale, in which it was decreed that bakers who short-changed their customers faced serious punishment – like having an arm chopped off. So, rather than risk such a fate, bakers would routinely hand over 13 items when asked for a dozen – just in case they'd miscounted or one of the items was defective in some way.

Have any famous people ever entered a competition to imitate or impersonate themselves – and lost?

Surprisingly, yes, they have! In an earlier book I told you how the great writer, Graham Greene, once entered a competition to parody his style in the *Spectator* and came third.

Well, now I've managed to find others!

The TV botanist David Bellamy was driving to an engagement one day, listening to a local radio station in his car. The station was running a phone-in for people to give their David Bellamy impersonation. He stopped at a telephone box, phoned in to take part – and – yup, you've guessed it – he too came third!

I'm not sure that this is absolutely true, but it has been claimed that the singer Elvis Presley entered an Elvis lookalike contest in a US burger joint and came third.

Interesting, isn't it, that it's always third – not second or fourth or nowhere – but third?

The only other people I can find who entered competitions to impersonate themselves – and lost! – are the singer and actress Dolly Parton and the actor Charlie Chaplin.

But then, I think it's extraordinary that there are *any*. I mean, can you imagine entering a competition to imitate yourself . . . and *not* winning? No, me neither!

How clever is your right foot?

This is a question – and answer – that was sent to me while I was writing this book. It's very funny – and true.

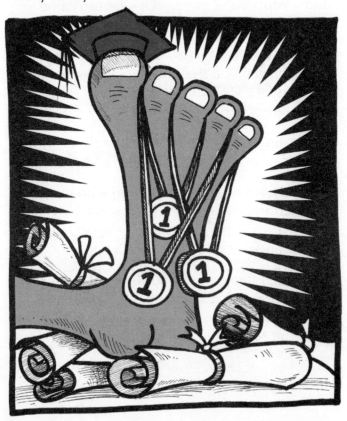

According to the person who sent it to me, it was devised by an orthopaedic surgeon. 'This will confuse your mind and you will keep trying over and over again to see if you can outsmart your foot, but you can't. It is pre-programmed in your brain!'

While sitting at your desk in front of your computer, lift your right foot off the floor and make clockwise circles.

Now, while doing this, draw the number 6 in the air with your right hand. Your foot will change direction.

I did it several times and, yes, my foot changed direction every time. Nice to know that I have no control over my own limbs!

If bats are blind, how do they manage to fly?

Good question . . . if only it were true! Bats aren't blind. They're not – honest! People think they are because they fly in the dark,

so it was assumed that they must be blind –
otherwise they'd fly in the light. But, in fact,
the reason they can fly in the dark is because
they have echo-location – a sort of radar –
which enables them to find their way even in
places (like caves) where there's no light.

However, most species of bat can see
perfectly well when it's light.

By the way, while we're exploding bat myths,
they DON'T get entangled in human hair and
very rarely transmit diseases to other animals
or humans.

How did the Frisbee get its name?

From a pie!

In the United States of the 1920s, students used to eat pies made by the Frisbie Pie Company of Bridgeport, Connecticut. When

the students had eaten the pies, they found that the empty pie tins could be thrown and caught – providing endless hours of fun. So they called these accidental toys 'Frisbies'.

The Wham-O company started making a commercial version and called it the Pluto Platter, but students persisted in calling it the Frisbie. So in 1957 the Wham-O company renamed their product the Frisbee.

When Neil Armstrong became the first man to step onto the moon, what did he say – and what did he *mean* to say?

At 2.56 a.m. – our time – on the morning of 21 July 1969, Neil Armstrong stepped onto the moon and uttered the words: 'That's one small step for man, one giant leap for mankind.' But if you think about it, that sentence is meaningless because of the omission of a single letter: the indefinite article 'a'. What he *meant* to say was: 'That's one small step for a man, one giant leap for mankind.' Otherwise the words 'man' and 'mankind' are interchangeable. Still, I suppose in the circumstances, he could be forgiven!

Interestingly, the phrase 'Neil Armstrong: That's one small step for a man, one giant leap for mankind' is a precise anagram of: 'Thin man ran; makes a large stride, left planet, pins flag on moon. On to Mars.'

Who first thought of using guide dogs to help the blind?

The earliest known example is probably the one depicted in a first-century (AD) mural in the buried ruins of Herculaneum, near Naples, in what is now Italy.

However, for the real origins of the Guide Dogs for the Blind movement, we have to go to Germany after the First World War, when thousands of soldiers were returning from the Front blinded, often by poison gas.

It was Dr Gerhard Stalling who is credited with this pioneering idea of training dogs to become reliable guides. In 1916 he opened the world's first guide dog school in Germany. Up to 600 dogs were trained every year until 1926, when it had to shut down. Another large guide dog centre was opened near Berlin, where they trained 100 dogs at a time. In its first 18 years, the school trained over 2,500 dogs, with a rejection rate of just 6 per cent.

Nowadays puppies are brought up for a year with a volunteer family, following puppy-walking guidelines. These include walking on the left-hand side of their handlers, and not to heel but a few paces in front; learning to ignore loud and unusual noises, including pneumatic drills and fire-engine sirens, and to cope with rush-hour crowds; and also (for obvious reasons) learning to relieve themselves on command.

Nearly 5,000 puppies are accepted each year for the training programmes, of which just over 3,000 pass the demanding process. After nine months of professional training the dog is introduced to its owner. They then spend several weeks together at a training centre getting used to each other. The biggest problem blind people face while training and when they return home is the threat of other dogs distracting the guide dogs.

This is a lengthy and expensive business. Each dog costs £35,000 on average, and each of Britain's 5,000 guide dog owners may have as many as six or seven animals in their lifetime.

Guide Dogs for the Blind keeps records

of each dog's parentage, appearance, temperament and health, together with assessments of their performance. A great deal of care goes into matching dogs with owners and their lifestyles – a keen walker will need a dog that doesn't suddenly decide to chase rabbits; a frequent flyer will need a dog that is relaxed in airports; and if a potential owner regularly attends church, they will want to be sure that the dog doesn't join in the singing.

How many oceans are there in the world?

This is not an easy question to answer. For just as oceans flow into one another, so do their names.

Talking of which, I have actually seen one of the places where the Pacific and Atlantic Oceans meet – and jolly unimpressive it was too!

Anyway, back to the question. There used to be four official oceans: the Arctic, the Atlantic, the Indian and the Pacific – or three for those who considered the Arctic a sea of the Atlantic. Then, in the year 2000, the International Hydrographic Organization (IHO) created the fifth from the Pacific, Atlantic and Indian Oceans where they flow *below* 60 degrees from the Equator – i.e. around Antarctica.

Two names were considered for this new ocean: the Southern Ocean and the Antarctic Ocean. The IHO asked its 68 member countries (membership being unavailable to landlocked countries) which name they preferred. Fewer than half the countries responded, but a majority voted in favour of calling it the Southern Ocean.

What's the most unusual 'luxury' chosen on *Desert Island Discs?*

Desert Island Discs is a long-running radio programme in which famous people are invited to talk about the eight songs or

pieces of music they would take with them to a desert island. In addition to the music, they're also allowed to select a luxury. Most 'castaways' (as guests are termed) choose perfectly sensible things like beds, pillows, baths, metal detectors, fishing rods, musical instruments – as well as food and drink.

However, some choose rather more unusual

'luxuries'. As I wrote in *Why Does Ear Wax Taste So Gross?* (available in all good book stores, etc., etc.), writer and film director Richard Curtis chose the Notting Hill Pizza Express. Other people who wanted specific buildings or places included opera singer Bryn Terfel (the Millennium Centre in Cardiff), former Prime Minister Sir John Major (The Oval cricket ground) and Sir Terry Pratchett (New York's Chrysler Building). Jacqueline Wilson (a fairground carousel) was no less demanding.

But all those luxuries were at least understandable – in contrast to . . .

A car to listen to music in (Sir Michael Gambon).

Virtual sherry trifle (writer and producer Armando Iannucci).

A television set that doesn't work (former police chief Sir Robert Mark).

Perhaps the most extraordinary request came from top golfer Colin Montgomerie – who asked for . . . 'nothing' as he's 'had enough luxury to last a lifetime'.

My luxury would be either a bed, a guitar, or, like the film director Mike Leigh, a loo and loo paper.

What would *yours* be?

Why do cartoon characters have just three fingers?

They do, you know. All of them from Mickey Mouse to Homer Simpson. In fact, now that I think about it, a cartoon character with the full complement of four fingers and a thumb would look ... odd. But presumably that's

only because we're so used to seeing them with a finger missing.

How did it start?

According to a cartoonist friend of mine, it is because it was simpler – 'Especially in the early days of animation, when everything had to be done by hand. Animators would have to draw thousands of pictures and it was easier to do characters with three fingers instead of four. Also, you have to remember that animation was a lot more basic in the beginning. They weren't trying to achieve precision; just a general sense of a character.'

Is it true that cats and dogs don't like each other?

This is a myth, perpetuated by cartoons characters like Garfield and Odie. In fact, most cats and dogs get along just fine – especially if they're introduced to each other when they're very young so they don't know any different. Ideally a cat should be under six months old and a dog under a year.

Researchers in Israel found that the

relationships work best if the cat is in the home before the dog arrives, rather than the other way round. Of course, if any cat or dog has had a bad experience with a dog or cat then it might well be wary of any others it meets. Also, there are some (thankfully not many) dogs that are so aggressive they can't even live with people, never mind other animals.

Is there – or was there – a Mr IKEA?

Sort of. IKEA, the furniture manufacturing and retail company, was founded in Sweden in 1943 by Ingvar Kamprad, who used his own initials and the first letters of Elmtaryd and Agunnaryd, the farm and town where he grew up, to form IKEA.

Why do we call the French 'frogs' – and what do they call us in return?

We call the French 'frogs' or 'froggies' because of the ancient French heraldic shield with three frogs painted on it. Also, we were somewhat appalled by the French habit of eating frogs' legs.

In return, they call us 'les rosbifs' – the roast beefs – which is what they imagine we eat all the time (especially overcooked).

The truth is, these days we all eat the same sort of food, but given the choice, I'd much rather have a plate of roast beef than a plate of frogs' legs.

While we're on the subject of frogs' legs, when I was 14 or 15, I went on an exchange trip to Rouen in Normandy. The delightful family who looked after me asked if there was any food I didn't eat. The only thing I could think of was frogs' legs, but I had absolutely no idea what the French was for 'frog'. The best I could come up with was: '*Je ne mange pas les jambes des petites bêtes vertes qui sautent,*' which translates as: 'I don't eat the legs of the little green beasts which jump.'

After much confusion – and no little embarrassment – they finally realized what I was on about. '*Ah,*' they said, '*les cuisses de grenouilles!*' (Literally, 'the thighs of frogs'.) Amid much laughter – none of it mine – they informed me that frogs' legs were an expensive delicacy and there was absolutely no way that I was going to be given them.

And I haven't eaten them to this day!

How rare are four-leaved clovers?

Surprisingly – given the myth that has grown up about them – not very rare at all. The rule of thumb is that there is at least one four-leaved clover in every 25 square centimetres of clover. Or, put another way, there are thought to be 10,000 three-leaved clovers for every four-leaved one. You just have to look for it!

Four-leaved clovers are reckoned to be lucky. In the Middle Ages a four-leaved clover was supposed to allow you to see – and even talk to – fairies.

So just how lucky is Edward Martin from Alaska, who has collected 160,000 four-leaved clovers? And that's without going to specialist farms in the US that specialize in growing thousands of four-leaved clovers, which are sealed in plastic as charms.

And what about nine-year-old Alastair Barnes, who in 2009 found a seven-leaved

clover close to his home in Coombe Bissett, near Salisbury in Wiltshire? He must be jolly lucky!

But not as lucky as the Japanese farmer who found a 21-leaved clover in 2000!

How many possible murderer/weapon/place combinations are there in a game of Cluedo?

Cluedo has six potential suspects, six possible weapons and nine different places where the murder could have been committed: 6 x 6 x 9 = 324. So there are 324 potential murder combinations, which explains why the game can be played repeatedly without players tiring of it.

Cluedo was invented by Anthony Pratt, a Midlands-based solicitor's clerk who retired just after the Second World War. He and his wife Marjorie were enthusiastic 'gamesters' who loved playing board games with their friends.

They invented the classic 'whodunnit' game

in 1944, and Mrs Pratt designed the board as the fictitious home of the victim, Dr Black. They played their home-made Cluedo with friends for three years, before they were urged to submit it to Waddingtons, the games manufacturer, for commercial mass-production.

The company liked the game immediately and launched it in 1948.

Over three million Cluedo games are sold every year around the world in more than a dozen different languages.

Are all snails edible?

I guess that depends on how hungry you are.

I've lived for many years without once being tempted to eat one – and frying them in garlic and calling them *escargots* doesn't fool me either.

Having said that, snails contain many nutrients, such as vitamins B1 and E, and are rich in calcium and low in calories and fat.

But even so . . .

Anyway, it turns out that they're NOT all edible, so DON'T start eating something you find in the garden. Not even for a dare.

The species that are most commonly eaten – though not, we've established, by the author – are *Helix aspersa* or *Helix pomatia*, although other varieties of snails are consumed.

Heli- is the prefix to all things snail, and that's why heliciculture is the name given to snail farming, which is a real industry (especially in France).

To summarize then. Snails: yeuch. Not even for a bet. However, if they're offered on a restaurant menu, then I suppose they're all right. But only if you really REALLY have to.

We're all familiar with collective names for animals – like a pride of lions, a pack of dogs or a colony of ants – but are there any really unusual ones?

Yes, there are some genuinely extraordinary ones. For some reason, flocks of birds attract the most unusual names:

A cast or kettle of hawks

A parliament of owls

A murder of crows

A charm of finches

An ascension or exultation of larks

A murmuration of starlings

A bevy, herd, lamentation or wedge of swans

A descent of woodpeckers

Moving on to different species/creatures, I like the fact that, as well as being known as a 'flight', a group of butterflies is also a 'rabble', and these others are also fun: a smack of jellyfish, a troubling of goldfish, a bloat of hippopotami, a rhumba of rattlesnakes and a mischief of mice.

And then there's another group of animals that take the collective name of 'herd' but also have some wonderful alternatives: an obstinacy of buffalo, a pace of donkeys, a parade of elephants, an implausibility of gnu and a crash of rhino.

Language can be a lot of fun!

Do you have to have a middle name?

No, you don't. It isn't a legal requirement and many people don't. Some people have several middle names – for example, the Mayor of London, Boris Johnson, has the full name Alexander Boris de Pfeffel Johnson – while others get by with just the one.

The first Englishman known to have a middle name was the Earl of Arundel, who in 1608 was baptized with the names Henry and Frederick. However, the expression 'middle name' wasn't used until at least 200 years later.

Nowadays, babies are often given middle names that honour older or deceased members of the family. Some are given their mother's maiden name just to keep that name alive.

There are no rules about middle names, and parents often just give their offspring ones that 'go' with their first names or can be used as alternatives if the children don't like their first names.

And then there are the parents who gave their subsequently famous children very unusual middle names. In *How to Avoid a Wombat's Bum*, I told you about Mel COLUMCILLE Gibson, Joseph ALBERIC Fiennes, Geri ESTOLLE Halliwell, John MARWOOD Cleese, Ben GEZA Affleck and Richard TIFFANY Gere.

Now consider these middle names:

Uma KARUNA Thurman

Rob HEPLER Lowe

Quincy DELIGHT Jones

Kate GARRY Hudson

Dom ROMULUS Joly

Nick WULSTAN Park

Spencer BONAVENTURE Tracy

Chris LIVINGSTONE Eubank

Alan WOLF Arkin

and Daniel WROUGHTON Craig.

Why are doctors sometimes called 'quacks'?

'Quack' is a rude word for a doctor – in much the same way that 'hack' is a derogatory term for a journalist. In fact, quack's worse than hack because it suggests wrongdoing as opposed to just uselessness.

The word quack – which is defined as 'a fraudulent or ignorant pretender to medical skill' – came from the old Dutch word 'quacksalver', for a person who sold their wares in a market by shouting about them. To quack meant to shout or boast, while a salve was a medical ointment.

So you can see why unscrupulous and possibly even bogus doctors would have become known as quacks.

What is the highest denomination bank note in circulation?

The largest bank note in circulation in all of Britain is the £50 note. There is also a £100 note, which is only available in Scotland, but that isn't used very often. The Scots also still have a £1 note – but, again, that's relatively rare.

Even rarer are the notes used internally

at the Bank of England (i.e. not actually in circulation), where they have one known as a Titan, which is worth £100 million.

That would be nice to find in a birthday card, wouldn't it?

Can you trust the Cretan who tells you that all Cretans are liars?

OK, I'm not stupid, I can work this out for myself without having to resort to professionals.

All right, he's either telling the truth or he's telling a lie.

If he's telling the truth, he must be a liar.

If he's lying, he's telling the truth.

Oops. I need help.

Still, apparently I'm not alone in being baffled by this. In his autobiography, the philosopher

Bertrand Russell recalled how he spent several months trying to solve it. Evidently he didn't have any mates to tell him to 'get a life'.

So I got in touch with my friend Stuart, who's got a degree in philosophy. 'Aha,' he said, 'the Liar's Paradox. I hope you're not losing sleep over it!'

Are you joking?

'Well, I did, and so did Bertrand Russell, who spent several—'

I know, I know, get on with it.

'OK, it is, of course, a meaningless, circular, illogical question – for reasons that you will have already worked out. However, there is a solution to it, which goes like this. Let's take all the things that Cretans say and then decide which statements are important and which ones aren't.

'When this Cretan says that all Cretans are liars, it only makes sense if we rank this statement above all other statements made by him or other Cretans.

'Yes, we know that Cretans always lie, but

this Cretan, on this occasion, is making what we call a "superior statement": he is, if you like, standing outside of his (for want of a better word) "Cretan-ness" and giving us an overview about Cretans. In other words, our Cretan friend is telling the truth. So, yes, you can believe him.'

NB This conundrum or paradox goes back centuries and has nothing to do with the good people of Crete, who are, I am sure, just as truthful as the rest of civilization!

When it comes to Comic Relief Red Nose Day, why don't people just keep their 'noses' from previous years rather than buying new ones?

Apart from the fact that it wouldn't be very charitable, it would also be deeply unfashionable. The people who run Comic

Relief cleverly change the design of the nose every time. Here are all the noses ever since it started:

1988: The Plain Red Nose

1989: The Smiley Face – with face made from rose-scented plastic

1991: The Stonker Nose – with hands and face

1993: The Tomato Nose – with stalk and face

1995: The Colour Change Nose – with MY NOSE on

1997: The Furry Nose – clear plastic shell covered in red fur

1999: The Big Red Hooter – faceless, gold glitter (when squeezed, it 'hooted')

2001: The Whoopee Nose – red head with inflated cheeks (when squeezed, the tongue inflated)

2003: The Big Hair-Do – with

gooey eyes that squeezed out

2005: Big Hair & Beyond – with smiley face and colourful elastic hair

2007: The Big One (The Nose That Grows) – made of foam (came with stickers, etc., with which to decorate the nose)

2009: There were three noses available:

Nose 1 (This One) had a big smile with mouth open;

Nose 2 (That One) had glasses on, and a smile with the teeth closed;

Nose 3 (The Other One) had a shocked look.

All three came with stickers depicting each of the noses, the logo and tag-line 'Do something funny for money'. A small book of nose-related jokes was also included.

Is it true that if it rains on St Swithin's Day (15 July), it will rain for a further 40 days and nights? And who was this St Swithin anyway?

St Swithin (or Swithun) was a ninth-century Bishop of Winchester who was renowned for his kindness to the poor. His association with rain comes about because he asked to be buried out of doors – so that 'the sweet rain from heaven may fall upon my grave' – rather than in his cathedral. This was enough to inspire the folklore about rain on St Swithin's Day.

Whether or not it's true ... well, why don't you take note of the weather next 15 July and see for yourself!

How long is a light-year?

The light-year is a measure of distance, not time. As such, it's the total distance that a beam of light, moving in a vacuum in a straight line, travels in one year (5.88 trillion miles). As for light itself, that travels at a constant speed of 186,000 miles per second. To give you an idea of just how fast this is, a traveller moving at the speed of light would circumnavigate the world at the Equator about seven times a second!

How come we don't fall out of bed when we're asleep?

Some people do – especially babies and very small children. That's why babies are put in cots and children have bed guards. It's also why young children aren't supposed to sleep in a top bunk in bunk-beds.

As you get older, though, you get to sense where the edge of the bed is and not to roll off it – even in your sleep. This means that older children and adults should never fall out of bed – unless they've drunk too much alcohol. So if you find one of your parents asleep on the floor in the morning, don't let them tell you that they fell out of bed, because you'll know better.

Why do we say 'That's the ticket!' when something is just right?

That comes from the American Depression of the 1930s, when millions of people were out of work and, in some cases, actually homeless and living on the streets.

Fortunately, there were soup kitchens which dispensed free soup and bread, but you had to have a meal ticket in order to get it – to stop people getting more than their fair share. So 'that's the ticket' became a saying meaning everything was fine.

Why is Friday the 13th considered to be unlucky?

The fear of the number 13 – or 'triskaidekaphobia', as it's technically known – goes back a long way. According to

Scandinavian mythology, there was a banquet in Valhalla gate-crashed by Loki (the god of strife) – thereby making 13 guests – where Balder (the god of light) was murdered. In Christian countries, this superstition was confirmed by the Last Supper, which had 13 attendees.

Meanwhile, Friday is considered unlucky because it was the day of the Crucifixion, and because Adam and Eve ate the forbidden fruit on a Friday and also died on a Friday. Some Buddhists and Brahmins (high-caste Hindus) also consider Friday to be unlucky. In combining superstitions about both Friday and the number 13, Friday the 13th is considered twice as frightful.

What's the most stupid thing that anyone's ever done?

Hmm, that's a tough one. There are many, many truly daft people in the world who do stupid things all the time.

Fortunately, for the sake of this question, there are the annual Darwin Awards – a tongue-in-cheek bit of tomfoolery – that seek to honour 'those who do a service to humanity by permanently removing themselves from the gene pool'. Here are some past deeds which have been 'recognized' by the judges:

Attempting to play Russian roulette with a semi-automatic pistol that automatically reloads the next round into the chamber.

Juggling active hand grenades.

Crashing through a window and falling to your death in trying to demonstrate that the window is unbreakable.

Jumping out of a plane to film skydivers,

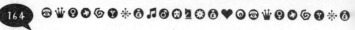

without wearing a parachute.

All pretty stupid, huh? However, the one that really takes the biscuit is 'Using a lighter to illuminate a fuel tank to make sure it contains nothing flammable.'

. . . And, following on from that, who's the most stupid criminal of all time?

Ooh, there's a tough contest! When it comes to daft actions, criminals seem to vie with each other to be the best.

You doubt me?

Well then, please consider the following before I divulge my all-time 'favourite'.

The burglar who left his mobile phone at the scene of the crime and then phoned it – only to give the police officer (who was in possession of it) his name and address.

The gang that tried breaking into a safe with what they thought were cutting tools but which were, in fact, welding tools. They had merely made the safe even safer.

The robber who threw a brick into the Plexiglas window of a jewellery store. Unfortunately for him, the brick bounced back, hit him on the head and knocked him out cold on the street, where he remained until the police got there.

The robber who went to a motel armed with an electric chainsaw. Alas for her, it wasn't much use as it wasn't plugged in.

The pair of robbers who entered a US music shop nervously waving guns. One of them shouted, 'Nobody move!' His partner moved and so he shot him.

The American robber who tried shooting someone during a hold-up. The gun failed to go off and so the robber peered down the barrel and tried it again. This time, it worked.

The man who was charged with stealing

money from vending machines: he pleaded 'not guilty' and then tried to pay for his bail in . . . coins.

The burglar who broke into a house to steal the TV but instead turned it on and began to watch it. Eventually, he fell asleep. When the householders came home, they found him and called the police.

The man who robbed a convenience store and fled with a pocket full of change. However, unbeknown to him, he had holes in both his pockets. A trail of coins led police directly to his home.

I also like the story of the man accused of a robbery who said he couldn't have done it because he was busy breaking into a school at the same time. So police arrested him for breaking into the school.

But my nomination for the most stupid criminal of all time has to be the man who robbed a US convenience store by putting a $20 bill on the counter and asking for change. When the shop assistant opened the till, the man pulled a gun and demanded all the cash in it. He ran away with all the cash – leaving the $20 bill on the counter. The total amount of cash he got from the till? $15. Which meant he had *given* the store $5. Now *that's* stupid.

How does Cockney rhyming slang work?

It's used – or at least it *was* used – to disguise meaning, as a sort of secret code.

So although you might hear a character in a TV programme say 'Look at his Barnet Fair'

meaning 'Look at his hair', a true Cockney would just say 'Look at his Barnet' – confident that the person they were talking to would get their meaning and the person they were talking about wouldn't.

Similarly 'apples' (short for 'apples and pears') means 'stairs', and 'trouble' (short for 'trouble and strife') means wife.

Does Donald Duck have a middle name?

Yes he does. It's Fauntleroy.

But it's probably the least interesting thing about this remarkable cartoon character who made his debut on 9 June 1934 in the Silly Symphony cartoon *The Wise Little Hen*.

He was created by Walt Disney after hearing Clarence Nash doing his 'duck' voice. Disney wanted a character who could portray some of the more negative traits that Mickey Mouse didn't have (especially a quick

temper). Donald was
voiced by Clarence 'Ducky'
Nash from 1934 to 1983, and after that
by Tony Anselmo.

The animation department in charge of
Donald never referred to him as Donald
Duck: they always called him 'The Duck'.

Donald's catchphrases include: 'This is very
exasperating,' 'Hiya, toots!', 'So!', 'That'll hold
ya!', 'This requires strategy,' and 'Oh, yeah?'

Donald usually wears a sailor shirt, cap, and a
red or black bow tie, but no trousers (except
when he goes swimming).

Donald Duck is particularly well-known and
popular in Scandinavian countries, where
voters placing 'protest votes' often write in
Donald Duck as the candidate.

Despite their huge rivalry, Donald is a VIP
member of the Mickey Mouse Club.

In 2005 Donald received a star on the Hollywood Walk of Fame. He is also the mascot for the University of Oregon.

What exactly is a leprechaun?

If you believe they exist, leprechauns are mischievous male fairies who live in Ireland. They're usually depicted as cobblers working on a single shoe. Although they're quite old, they're no taller than a small child and have a stash of buried treasure. According to myth, you may find a leprechaun and his pot of gold at the end of a rainbow. Also, if you keep your eye fixed on a leprechaun, he can't escape, but the moment you look away, he vanishes.

Is it true that lightning never strikes twice?

No it's not. In fact, the opposite is the case: lightning is much *more* likely to strike again where it has struck before. Why? Because lightning tends to strike the tallest object around, so tall buildings, bridges, trees, etc., get many repeated strikes.

However, steps can be taken to ensure that lightning doesn't strike twice by protecting buildings and bridges with lightning conductors, which absorb the lightning and discharge it safely into the ground.

Why is £1000 known as 'a grand'?

It started off as American slang for $1,000 at the start of the 20th century. It came to Britain during the Second World War (1939–45), when many Americans were stationed over here.

The origins aren't certain but it probably derives from the idea that 1,000 (dollars or pounds) is a 'grand sum'.

Nowadays, the word 'grand' is used to mean 1,000 of anything and not just currency.

Why can't we eat grass?

Actually, you *can* eat grass and, especially on a sunny day, there will be some sugars in it that you can absorb, but you can't use the cellulose that makes up most of the calories, so you would have to eat a huge amount to derive any benefit, and that would make you feel very unwell.

Human stomachs have difficulty digesting raw leaves and grasses. Animals like cows, on the other hand, have four stomachs to help them digest grass (a process called rumination, in which they bring the grass back up to chew it a second time, known as 'chewing the cud'. That's why we call animals like horses, sheep, rabbits and goats that graze on grass *ruminant* animals. They all have complex guts that involve a fermentation stage where they grow bacteria to break down the cellulose into sugars that can then be absorbed. This is also why rabbits eat some of their own soft droppings).

Apart from the digestion problem, another difficulty for us when it comes to eating grass is mastication or chewing. Grass contains a lot of silica, an abrasive which quickly wears down teeth. Ruminant animals have teeth that are adapted to grow continually, quickly replacing the worn surfaces. Indeed, if you don't give a pet rabbit something hard to chew on like a lump of wood, its teeth will grow so long it won't be able to eat any food at all.

Why was the word 'the' once represented as 'ye'?

It still is in villages that pride themselves on being tourist attractions. How often have you seen cafés, for example, calling themselves 'Ye Olde Worlde Tea Shoppe'?

Of course, our immediate instinct is to pronounce the 'ye' as 'yee' but we would be wrong. It should actually be pronounced 'the'. The Romans related the 'th' sound to the

word 'thorn'. So far so reasonable. But then they looked for a letter that most resembled a thorn, and it was the lower case y.

And that's how you get 'ye' and, thinking about it, the opposite is true, with 'thou' being used for 'you'.

No wonder foreigners have such trouble with our language!

Why are people's eyes different colours?

It is, of course, genetic: we inherit eye and hair colour from our parents or grandparents.

But they, in turn, will have inherited those colours from *their* parents, and if you go back far enough, it's all down to the way in which those distant ancestors adapted to the climate they lived in. Dark pigment in the eyes and skin protects against the damaging rays of the bright sun. Lighter pigment allows the skin to absorb more sunlight, ideal for areas with little sun. So what you look like today depends in large part on what your ancestors encountered centuries ago.

Is it possible for a person to have two eyes of different colours?

Yes it is. The medical term is *Heterochromia iridium* and it's the condition of having two different-coloured eyes due to uneven melanin (pigment) content.

However, it's very rare – although each of

the following celebrities has eyes of different colours:

Jane Seymour (one green and one brown)

David Bowie (one green and one blue)

Christopher Walken (blue/hazel)

Kiefer Sutherland (blue/green)

Kate Bosworth (blue/brown)

Why do squirrels have fluffy tails?

My immediate reaction was to say, 'Because it makes them look cute.' And who can deny that squirrels have much better PR than rats and mice, which don't have fluffy tails?

After some research, I discovered that there is, in fact, a perfectly good evolutionary reason why squirrels have acquired their thick tails.

A squirrel's paws are like Velcro, so they can

cling onto things like branches or roof tiles without falling down. Because of this, they spend a lot of time jumping through the air. Consequently, they need the extra stability that having a tail gives them while they're jumping.

Rats and mice, on the other hand, are ground dwellers and so they don't need fluffy tails.

Even though they would look so much cuter with them.

Where is the precise centre of England?

In 2002 an Ordnance Survey map identified Lindley Hall Farm, near Fenny Drayton, Leicestershire, as the centre of England.

What sort of products are available to people who are left-handed?

The short answer is: all the products that are available to right-handed people! However, I take it that the questioner wants to know if there are *specific* products for those of us who are left-handed.

The good news is that there are plenty of them!

In fact, there's a specialist shop in London called the Anything Left-Handed Shop (it also has a website) where they sell any number of things for lefties. And not just the obvious

things like scissors, but also boomerangs
(which have the wing profile machined for
left-handed throwing), calculators (specially
made to fit in the right hand and be operated
by the fingers of the left hand), watches (the
adjustment winder is positioned on the left-
hand side of the face so that it can be worn
on the right wrist), mugs (have a slogan that
shows away from the drinker only if held in
the left hand), pencil sharpeners (the pencil
is held in the left hand and turned anti-
clockwise), corkscrews (have a screw which
turns anti-clockwise – the natural way for a
left-hander), rulers (scaled from right to left,
making it easy to draw lines of the correct
length with the left hand without obscuring
the scale at the same time), desk/wall
clocks (these run anti-clockwise, the natural
direction for left-handers), milk/cream jugs

(these have lips at 'left-angles' so that they only pour conveniently from the left hand) and calendars (with the months and the days running from right to left).

Having said that, this left-hander finds that he can manage perfectly well with right-handed products – if only because I've always had to. Indeed, when my bank manager realized I was left-handed and sent me a left-handed chequebook, I had to send it back because I couldn't adjust to it!

What's the meaning of the nursery rhyme 'Here We Go Round the Mulberry Bush'?

You probably know this one. It starts with the chorus:

Here we go round the mulberry bush,
The mulberry bush, the mulberry bush.
Here we go round the mulberry bush
On a cold and frosty morning.

Then the verses start:

This is the way we wash our clothes,
Wash our clothes, wash our clothes.
This is the way we wash our clothes
On a cold and frosty morning.

This is the way we iron our clothes,
Iron our clothes, iron our clothes.
This is the way we iron our clothes
On a cold and frosty morning.

This is the way we scrub the floor,
Scrub the floor, scrub the floor.
This is the way we scrub the floor
On a cold and frosty morning.

And on it goes for several verses.

So what does it all mean – if anything? The origins are really rather dark as the song derives from the middle of the 19th century when female prisoners at Wakefield Jail used to entertain their children by walking around a mulberry bush within the prison area and then singing about that and all the chores they had to do.

Apart from the colour, is there any difference between white and brown eggs?

According to the expert I consulted (my wife, Penny, who keeps chickens that lay delicious eggs), 'There is absolutely no difference in taste or nutrition between white and brown eggs. They simply come from different breeds of chickens.'

So why do many people prefer brown eggs?

'It goes back to the days when commercial farmers only sold white eggs, so you could only get brown eggs from farm shops and these tasted better because they came from free-range hens. There's no doubt that free-range eggs taste better than eggs from battery chickens – quite apart from the issue of animal welfare.

'Nowadays, the colour of the egg is meaningless: all that matters is whether or not the chickens are free range and are well fed. If they are, you get bright-yellow yolks that taste heavenly; if they're not, the yolks will be wishy-washy and taste of nothing.'

What's the most unusual name given to a child by a celebrity?

In previous books I've listed some of the unusual – not to say daft – names given to children by celebrities. Names such as Princess Tiaamii (the name given to their

daughter by Katie Price and Peter Andre),
Apple (Gwyneth Paltrow and Chris Martin),
Dusti Rain and KeeLee Breeze (Vanilla Ice),
Moon Unit, Dweezil and Diva (Frank Zappa),
and four sons named George (George
Foreman).

Here are some other, er, 'different' names
chosen by the famous for their poor
offspring:

Elijah Blue and Chastity Sun (Cher)

Satchel (Woody Allen)

Willow (Gabrielle Anwar)

Camera (Arthur Ashe)

Free (Barbara Hershey and
David Carradine)

Braison Chance and
Destiny Hope (Billy Ray
Cyrus – the father of Miley
Cyrus)

Petal Blossom Rainbow, Poppy Honey and
Daisy Boo (Jamie Oliver)

Denim (Toni Braxton)

and Sunday (Nicole Kidman)

All satisfyingly bonkers, I think you'll agree, but which one deserves the award for the most awful?

It's a close call, but I think it has to go to the excellent Oscar-winning actor, Forest Whitaker, who named his three children True, Ocean and Sonnet. If that's not bad enough, he also has a stepdaughter (who, presumably, he didn't name) called . . . Autumn.

Very strange . . .

Why is yellow the colour of cowardice?

Yellow has always been associated with cowardice and treachery. Judas Iscariot, the apostle who betrayed Jesus Christ, is almost always painted wearing yellow in medieval paintings. In Spain, victims of the Inquisition wore yellow, to imply they were guilty of heresy and treason. In the American Wild

West, a man thought to be cowardly was called a 'yellow-belly' or a 'yellow dog'.

But why yellow? Almost certainly, we're back in the area of the four 'humours' (see *Why is green the colour of envy?*). Too much yellow bile supposedly made you ill, unpleasant and pathetic – the sort of mood (and colour) that indicated a lack of willingness to behave in a strong manly way. From there, you can see why yellow would have become the colour of cowardice.

Well, one colour had to – so why not yellow?

Mind you, there are an awful lot of horrible things associated with the colour yellow. Quarantine (where people have to be kept away from other people because of their illness) is just the first that springs to mind.

Then there's yellow fever (an illness spread by mosquitoes, also known as *yellow jack*), yellow lines (places where you can't park – double and single), yellow journalism (sensational stories run to increase newspaper circulation). Even the Yellow Brick Road in *The Wizard of Oz* turned out to be not altogether nice.

The only positive uses of yellow would seem to be the yellow jersey (worn by the leading cyclist in the Tour de France), The Beatles' 'Yellow Submarine' (get your mum or dad to sing it for you), and the telephone directory for goods and services, the Yellow Pages.

Poor old yellow!

How do baby birds breathe inside eggs?

An eggshell may look solid, but it actually has nearly 8,000 pores that are large enough for oxygen to get in and carbon dioxide – i.e. what the birds are exhaling – to get out.

Why do dogs bark even before someone knocks at the door?

First of all, we have to understand *why* dogs bark when there's someone at the door. They bark to warn us, their owners, and they do this because they are pack animals and they see us – humans – as members of their pack. If you've got the relationship right, then they see you as leaders of the pack: woe betide

you if the dog thinks that *it's* the leader.

Secondly, the reason why they can anticipate a knock at the door is because their sense of hearing is at least 10 times more acute than a human's. They're helped in this by having twice as many muscles for moving their ears as we do. They can also detect sounds and sense frequencies at a far higher rate than we can.

Add to this their much more powerful sense of smell and you can see why we depend on them so much to warn us of potential upcoming danger.

However, although they fare better than us in two of the five senses (smell and sound), we do better than them in another two (sight and touch). This leaves taste, which, when it comes to ranking dogs and humans, doesn't really matter very much.

These different but equal abilities go to show why a dog really is man's best friend!

Is it true that Archimedes discovered his principle of displacement in the bath?

EUREKA!

Yes, and he was so excited by his discovery that he ran through the streets – naked – shouting 'Eureka!' (Meaning 'I have found it!')

Archimedes of Syracuse was a third-century BC Greek mathematician, physicist, engineer, inventor and astronomer.

According to legend – and so it's possible it might not be true – the reason why he needed to discover the principle that bears his name is because a laurel wreath had been made for King Hiero II, and Archimedes was asked to determine whether it was of solid gold or whether cheaper metals had been added by a dishonest goldsmith. While taking his bath, Archimedes noticed that the level

of the water in the bath rose as he got in, and realized that this effect could be used to determine the volume or density of the crown. In other words, just like a submerged man, the submerged crown would displace an amount of water equal to its own volume.

By dividing the weight of the crown by the volume of water displaced, he could discover if the density was lower than that of gold, which would indeed prove that other, less dense metals had been added.

No wonder Archimedes was so pleased with himself.

I am no scientist but, like Archimedes, I too have made valuable discoveries in the bath.

Such as . . .

The hot water always runs out just before you rinse your hair.

The shower attachment never gives you the correct mix of hot and cold water.

It is only when you actually sit down in the bath that you realize that the soap is in the basin.

However carefully you position the bathmat, water always goes on the floor.

However clean you leave a bath, it is always dirty the next time you go to use it.

If your phone is going to ring during your bath, it will happen precisely 30 seconds after you have fully submerged your body.

Remembering to put your towel on the radiator increases the likelihood of getting shampoo in your eyes.

Turning the taps on with your toes requires one and a half times as much effort as leaning forward to do it with your fingers.

Why do we describe someone who's being unrealistic as 'living in cloud-cuckoo-land'?

This comes from a play, *The Birds*, written by the Greek dramatist Aristophanes in 414 BC. One of his characters decides to build a perfect city between the clouds, to be named Cloud-Cuckoo-Land. The play was first translated into English in 1824 and you can see why, ever since, people have disparaged other people's dreams by telling them they're living in cloud-cuckoo-land.

What's the most extraordinary bequest ever made in a will?

There's a lot of competition here! But having done some research, I've come up with the following nominations:

In 1765 John Hart left his brother a gun and a bullet 'in the hope that he will put the same through his head when the money is spent'.

The British dramatist Richard Brinsley Sheridan told his son that he was cutting him out of his will with just a shilling. His son's reaction was, 'I'm sorry to hear that, sir. You don't happen to have the shilling about you now, do you?'

Heinrich Heine, the German poet, left everything to his wife on the condition that she remarried 'so that there will be at least one man to regret my death'.

In 1937 F. Scott Fitzgerald drew up a will in which he specified 'a funeral and burial in keeping with my station in life'. Three years later, just before his death, a much poorer Fitzgerald amended this provision to read 'cheapest funeral . . . without undue ostentation or unnecessary expense' – his funeral cost precisely $613.25.

The longest will in the world was one drawn up for Frederica Cook, an American woman – when it was approved at London's Somerset House in 1925, it consisted of four bound volumes totalling 95,940 words. Amazingly, she didn't have all that much to leave.

The shortest valid British will – which was contested but eventually passed after the 1906 case Thorne v. Dickens – consisted of three words: 'All for mother.' What caused the confusion was that the testator (the person who made the will) didn't mean his mother but his wife.

William Shakespeare bequeathed to his wife, Anne, 'my second best bed'. This has been interpreted as a snub. In fact, his 'second best bed' was probably the one most used by the two of them and it was therefore a sentimental gesture. His best bed went to the male heirs of his elder daughter, Susanna.

P. T. Barnum, the famous American showman, drew up a will in 1882 leaving his daughter, Helen, $1,500 a year for life. When she left her husband, Barnum wrote her out of the will. Then, in an 1889 codicil, he left her a property in Colorado which he believed was worthless. Two years later, he died and Helen inherited this property: it turned out to have mineral deposits which made her wealthier than all the other beneficiaries of Barnum's will *combined*.

In 1964 Ian Fleming, the author of the James Bond novels, left £500 to each of four friends with the instruction that they should 'spend the same within twelve months of receipt on some extravagance'.

A wealthy American banker left a codicil in his will cutting out two members of his family: 'To my wife and her lover, I leave the knowledge I wasn't the fool she thought I was. To my son, I leave the pleasure of earning a living. For twenty-five years he thought the pleasure was mine.'

However, the winner of the prize for the most extraordinary bequest ever made must go to Charles Millar, a Canadian lawyer who died in 1928 at the age of 73. Millar had a bizarre sense of humour and wondered how much people would do in the pursuit of money. To a preacher and a judge, who were both against gambling, he left shares in a racetrack that would make both men automatic members of a horse-racing club. Both accepted. To a group of ministers who were anti-alcohol, Millar left $50,000 worth of shares in a brewery – they all accepted bar one. To three acquaintances who loathed

each other, Millar bequeathed a holiday home in Jamaica which they were obliged to share – which they did. Most controversially, Millar bequeathed more than $500,000 to the Toronto woman who 'has given birth to the greatest number of children at the expiration of ten years from my death'. Millar's relatives tried – but failed – to overturn the will and, 10 years later, four women who had each had nine children in the 10 years shared the money.

In his will, Noah gave the whole world to his three sons – now *that's* what I call a bequest!

Why do dogs shake and chew things and bury bones?

Mostly because they're bored – but also to exercise themselves. Dogs also chew up your clothes because they want to smell like you. Shaking things viciously is also part of the hunting ritual. Lap dogs are less likely to do this sort of thing than the larger and more active breeds.

They bury bones because it is part of a dog's instinctive feeding ritual; even though they are fed regularly as pets, their wild genes make them plan ahead for times when there will be no more food, so burying a bone (or something else) is like us putting something somewhere safe for a rainy day (like pocket money?).

What's the funniest country & western song title?

Oh gosh, there's so much choice! Either deliberately or accidentally (and it's very often the former!), country & western songwriters do pick the most ludicrous titles for their songs. Here are my favourites:

'You're the Reason Our Kids Are Ugly' (Loretta Lynn)

'The Lord Knows I'm Drinkin'' (Cal Smith)

'You Just Hurt My Last Feeling' (Sammi Smith)

'She's Actin' Single (I'm Drinkin' Doubles)' (Gary Stewart)

'Heaven's Just a Sin Away' (The Kendells)

'I Forgot More Than You'll Ever Know' (The Davis Sisters)

'I'm Gonna Hire a Wino to Decorate Our Home' (David Frizzell)

Is it true that William Shakespeare died on his birthday?

It is said that Shakespeare was born on 23 April 1564 and died on the same date in 1616. If it's true, it would be wonderfully symmetrical – and so very English as that's also St George's Day.

However, there is some doubt over his precise date of birth. What we *do* know for sure is that he was baptized on 26 April, so

it's possible that he was born on the 23rd as babies were baptized very quickly in those days for fear that they would die beforehand and therefore be condemned to an eternity in limbo.

In any event, his date of death is certain and, given that there is this doubt over his birth date, it might as well be the 23rd as any other date. Which would mean that, yes, he died on his birthday.

Despite extensive research, I could find very few other famous people who died on their birthdays. Here are some examples:

Artist Raphael (6 April 1483–1520 – and for good measure both days fell on Good Friday)

Artist Frans Francken (6 May 1581–1642)

Football Manager Joe Mercer (9 August 1914–90)

Actress Ingrid Bergman (29 August 1915–82)

West Indian cricketer Keith Boyce (11 October 1943–96)

Ballerina Maria Taglioni (23 April 1804–84)

What are the worst noises in the world?

There is no definitive list, but please allow me to nominate the following:

The noise of fingernails scratching a blackboard.

The noise of someone taking their first violin lesson.

The noise of an ultra-sensitive car alarm.

The noise of a fly trapped in the bedroom when you're trying to sleep.

The noise of someone else's poorly tuned radio.

Has any one person ever won the Eurovision Song Contest more than once?

Just one person has. In 1987 Johnny Logan of Ireland became the only act to win twice – having won it before in 1980. On the same night, the German group Wind became the only act to finish second on two occasions.

Interestingly, Logan had a third victory to celebrate in 1992, when Linda Martin won the contest with 'Why Me?', a song which he composed.

What's the oddest book ever published?

That's hard to say, unless you have a list of every book ever published, which I don't. However, every year at the London Book Fair, one of the most eagerly awaited awards is the

Bookseller (the trade magazine of the book world) prize for the oddest title of the year. Here are some of the previous winners:

The 2009–2014 World Outlook for 60-milligram Containers of Fromage Frais
Proceedings of the Second International Workshop on Nude Mice

The Theory of Lengthwise Rolling

The Book of Marmalade: Its Antecedents, Its History, and Its Role in the World Today

Versailles: The View from Sweden

How to Avoid Huge Ships

Highlights in the History of Concrete

Greek Rural Postmen and Their Cancellation Numbers

Living with Crazy Buttocks

People Who Don't Know They're Dead: How They Attach Themselves to Unsuspecting Bystanders and What to Do About It

The Stray Shopping Carts of Eastern North America: A Guide to Field Identification

Are grasshoppers and crickets the same?

Er, no. That's why they have different names – but, to be fair to the questioner, they are remarkably similar, with almost identical body structures, including jumping hind legs. The basic difference between them is not so much physiological as behavioural: grasshoppers are active in the day while crickets are active at night.

How long does our queen – Elizabeth II – have left to reign before she becomes the longest-serving British monarch?

The longest-reigning British (or English) monarch since 1066 was Queen Victoria, who was on the throne for 64 years (from 1837–1901). The next longest was King George III (60 years: 1760–1820). Queen Elizabeth II lies in third place, having reigned since 1952 and having overtaken King Henry III (56 years: 1216–72) in 2008.

Queen Elizabeth needs to reign until 2012 to move ahead of King George III, and until 2016 to overhaul Queen Victoria.

What are the world's deadliest creatures?

OK, first a health warning: after you've read this you will never want to go anywhere exotic – especially Australia! In fact, climb under your duvet and hide, for the world has some truly horrible creatures – and some of their bites or stings have no known antidote. You have been warned!

First, however, I should explain that there is a difference between poisonous and venomous animals. A poisonous animal carries harmful chemicals called toxins, primarily used for

self-defence – whereas venomous animals deliver their toxins by stinging, stabbing, or biting. So poisonous animals are passive killers, while venomous animals are active killers. Thousands of animals use highly venomous or toxic poisons to attack prey or defend themselves.

These are the deadliest creatures in the world. Avoid them at all costs!

Box Jellyfish

This dangerous animal has caused at least 5,570 recorded deaths since 1954. Thankfully, it goes out of its way to avoid other creatures, but it can be found in quite large numbers in the oceans of Asia and Australia.

Box jellyfish venom is so awesomely painful that human victims go into severe shock and die of heart or lung failure before they can reach the shore. After a sting from one of these, you have virtually no chance of survival unless you are treated immediately. Vinegar is a good treatment which should be applied for a minimum of 30 seconds. Vinegar contains acetic acid, which disables the box jellyfish's toxins that have not yet discharged into the bloodstream (though it will not alleviate the pain). Survivors experience pain for weeks after contact with 'box jellies' (as the Aussies call them) as the venom will slowly eat away at the skin.

King Cobra

This is the world's longest venomous snake – growing up to 5.6m in length. Its Latin name,

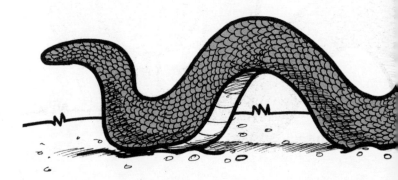

Ophiophagus, literally means 'snake-eater' as it eats other snakes. One single bite from this deadly snake can easily kill a human. It can even kill a fully-grown Indian elephant within three hours if it bites a vulnerable area like the trunk. King cobras can be found across South and South-east Asia, but thankfully they live in dense highland forests.

If a king cobra's venom is not quite as toxic as that of other venomous snakes, it has rather a lot of it: a king cobra is capable of injecting five times more venom than a black mamba, so it can kill five times faster.

Marbled Cone Snail

One drop of its venom is so powerful that it can kill more than 20 humans, though its true purpose is to catch prey. Although there is no antidote, there have only been around 30 recorded deaths.

The symptoms of a cone-snail sting can start immediately or may take days to develop. It results in intense pain, swelling, numbness and tingling. Severe cases involve muscle paralysis, numbness, nausea, changes in vision, lung failure and death. Though very slow moving, this snail thrives in warm-water reefs throughout the world.

Blue-ringed Octopus

The distinctively marked blue-ringed octopus – as found in tidal pools in the Pacific Ocean, from Japan to Australia – is actually very small, about the size of a golf ball, but its venom is so lethal that it can kill a human. Actually, it carries enough poison to kill 26 adult humans within minutes, and there is no antidote. Its painless bite may seem harmless, but the deadly neurotoxins begin working immediately, resulting in muscular weakness and numbness, followed by the cessation of breathing and, ultimately, death.

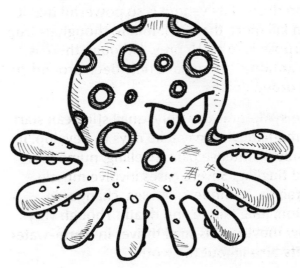

Death Stalker Scorpion

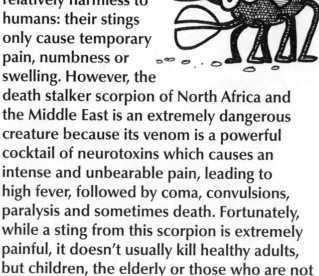

Contrary to popular belief, even though they look scary, most scorpions are relatively harmless to humans: their stings only cause temporary pain, numbness or swelling. However, the death stalker scorpion of North Africa and the Middle East is an extremely dangerous creature because its venom is a powerful cocktail of neurotoxins which causes an intense and unbearable pain, leading to high fever, followed by coma, convulsions, paralysis and sometimes death. Fortunately, while a sting from this scorpion is extremely painful, it doesn't usually kill healthy adults, but children, the elderly or those who are not well might all die.

Stonefish

The stonefish can be found in the shallow tropical marine waters of the Pacific

and Indian Oceans. It's quite deadly but, unfortunately for its victims, looks remarkably like a sea rock or coral. With its impressive camouflage, it attacks many fish that swim nearby. A powerful toxin stored

 within its 13 spines can stop almost any animal it touches. In humans, the venom will cause intense pain, swelling of tissue and shock, followed by death.

Its venom causes such agony that victims have described it as the worst pain known to man. Some want the affected limb to be amputated. If victims are not given medical attention within a couple of hours, the venom can be fatal.

Sydney Funnel Web Spider

Only found in Sydney, Australia (the clue is in the name), and named because of its unusual funnel-shaped webs, the funnel web spider is large (up to 7cm) and very aggressive, with the most powerful venom of any spider. From its fangs, the spider delivers a powerful neurotoxin that causes extreme pain and is capable of killing a person within 15 minutes. Interestingly, its

venom doesn't affect most other mammals but has a very powerful effect on humans. There is an antidote, but it has to be administered immediately after a bite to be effective.

I've just got back from Sydney and I kept a very close eye out for them during my trip!

Brazilian Wandering Spider

Sometimes known as the banana spider, this is the spider responsible for the most human deaths and is believed to have the

most potent neurotoxic venom of any spider.
Just 0.006mg is sufficient to kill a mouse.
They are particularly dangerous because they
frequently hide inside houses, clothes, boots
and cars in highly populated areas of Brazil.

Inland Taipan

This Australian snake is regarded by many
as the most poisonous on the planet. One
quick bite contains enough toxins to kill over
100 people. Its venom causes vomiting and
can stop a human victim from breathing.
Fortunately, although its venom is at least
200–400 times more toxic than a common
cobra's, the taipan is a very gentle and shy
reptile and rarely bites. When it does, it
hasn't proved fatal because there's an anti-
venom.

Poison Dart Frog

This small frog is probably the most poisonous creature on earth. At only 5cm long, it has enough venom to kill 10 people or 20,000 mice. Only 2 micrograms of its lethal toxin (the amount that fits on the head of a pin) is capable of killing a human or other large mammal. They were called 'dart frogs' because the indigenous Amerindians of Central and South America once used their toxic secretions to poison the tips of their blow-darts. Their bodies make the poison when they eat fire ants. We know this because, interestingly, if their diet in captivity doesn't include these ants, then they don't produce the venom.

Puffer Fish

Almost as poisonous as the dart frog is the puffer fish. Unbelievably, the meat of some species is considered a delicacy in both

Japan and Korea, but the problem is that the skin and certain organs of many puffer fish are very poisonous to humans. Most deaths from eating these fish occur when untrained people deal with them. As the poison can cause near instantaneous death, only licensed chefs are allowed to prepare them.

The puffer's poison causes deadening of the tongue and lips, dizziness, vomiting, rapid heart rate, difficulty breathing, and muscle paralysis. Victims die from suffocation as their diaphragm muscles are paralysed. Most of them die after four to 24 hours. There is no known antidote.

Call me a coward but, personally, I think I won't take the risk – I'll go for the cod and chips instead.

Why do bees sting us when the very act of stinging kills them?

They don't do it for fun, you know – only in self-defence. Which is why, when a bee comes near you, the worst thing you can do is scream and shout or, even worse, try to swat it! If you, and everyone near you, can keep perfectly still, the bee will almost always mind its own business and fly away.

Basically, bees will only sting you if they are provoked because, as I've already said in the question, stinging means their certain death.

Let me explain why: their sting has barbs, which allow it to enter the skin to inject their bite in a screwdriver action, but they can't get them out again.

And let's face it, we're not exactly going to help them to retract their sting, are we? We're going to be brushing it off as fast as we can.

The bee, however, is dead without its sting.

Interestingly, experienced beekeepers rarely get stung; when they are, they try to let the bee withdraw its sting so it can fly off unharmed.

By the way, if you are unlucky enough to be stung by a bee, don't use tweezers to remove the sting and don't try to squeeze it out, as this will only help the poison spread under the skin. The best thing to do is scrape it off with your fingernail or a credit card.

Surely cats don't *really* have nine lives?

Obviously not!

So why do people say they have?

It's probably to do with the fact that cats seem to have a remarkable ability to get out of trouble and can fall from great heights without any harm.

Humans have a reflex that helps us stay balanced. It's called the righting reflex.

This works so well that you may not even have noticed it – but when you are walking and you trip, immediately, a number of muscles in your legs, your back – maybe even your shoulders – suddenly work to try to keep your body upright.

Cats have *brilliant* righting reflexes. If a cat starts to fall, it rapidly twists its whole body in mid air and lands on its feet. In this way, cats often survive falls that would kill most other animals. This, combined with their small size and low body weight, helps to soften the impact as they make contact with the ground after falling.

But it's not only their righting reflex: cats also have highly developed inner ears which give them an unusually good sense of balance, which is critical to their landing on

their feet. This sense of balance allows a cat falling upside-down to right itself by rapidly determining its position, repositioning itself, and making any adjustments necessary to ensure that it lands on all four legs – thus ensuring that the impact is spread between them. Additionally, cats bend their legs when they land, which cushions the impact by spreading it, not only through bones that could easily break, but through the joints and muscles as well.

But that still doesn't answer the question. Why *nine* lives – why not eight or ten?

The answer probably lies in the idea that nine is a uniquely 'lucky' number: a trinity of trinities (i.e. 3 x 3) and a mystical number often invoked in religion and folklore.

And when did this feline association with the number nine start?

Almost certainly in ancient Egypt, where the cat was so revered that when one died, its owner would have it mummified and bury it with mummified mice. The owner would also shave off his eyebrows to show his grief!

Why are pirates depicted with a parrot on their shoulder?

Although piracy itself goes back thousands of years, the roots of the parrot-on-the-shoulder look can be firmly tracked back to the 19th century and Robert Louis Stevenson. He was, of course, the man who wrote *Treasure Island* and created the character of Long John Silver, the one-legged pirate with a parrot on his shoulder.

Treasure Island was such a success that (almost) every pirate book/film/play ever since has featured a pirate – often the captain – with a parrot on his shoulder.

However, there is at least some historical basis for Stevenson's creation. Pirates – and indeed ordinary sailors – who visited tropical lands often brought home exotic creatures as souvenirs. Parrots were particularly popular because they were colourful and could be taught to speak. They could also be sold for a lot of money.

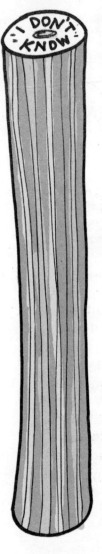

How do they get the letters into sticks of seaside rock?

At the start of the rock-making process, the rock is rolled out flat. It's at this point that the lettering is added. It could be anything – from the name of a seaside town to a person's name to something very rude!

Rock is still made by hand and it's quite difficult to make, which is why it is relatively expensive.

When and where did skateboarding start?

Skateboarding first started on the west coast of California in the 1950s. It came about because

surfers
wanted to
surf the streets. No
one knows who made the first
board: in fact, almost certainly lots of
people developed boards at the same time.

Those first skateboards were wooden boxes
with roller-skate wheels on the bottom.
Soon, planks were used instead of boxes, and
eventually companies were producing decks
of wood to be used as skateboards.

Is it true that animals can only see in black and white?

It depends on the animal. Some animals can see some colours; some can't. The ones that can see colours don't necessarily see the same colours as we do. Monkeys, squirrels, birds, insects and many fish can see a fairly good range of colours – maybe not as good as us but better than cats and dogs.

Horses, for example, see most colours as shades of grey, but they can see blues. Dogs

can't distinguish between red and green (what we would call colour-blind) but they *can* distinguish between blue and yellow. *Most birds, on the other hand, can see even more* colours than we can: imagine how beautiful a (male) peacock must look to a (lady) peahen!

However, at this point I should explain that bulls are, in fact, colour-blind. Even though matadors always use a red cape in bullfights, the bull doesn't see it as red. The bull only charges the red cape because it is moving, not because it's red.

What makes white chocolate white?

White chocolate is produced using the same process as milk chocolate and dark chocolate. The difference is in the ingredients.

Chocolate comes from the cacao tree, which grows in equatorial areas of South America, Africa and Asia. The seeds of the tree's fruits are the cocoa beans, which are harvested, fermented for six or seven days, and then

dried. The best-quality chocolate comes from cocoa beans that are dried naturally in the sun for a week; shorter, artificial drying yields inferior chocolate. Next, the beans are roasted and the shells removed. Then the cocoa is ground, resulting in a thick liquid called chocolate liquor (it's not alcoholic). This liquor is pressed to extract the fat, which is called cocoa butter. With the fat removed, the liquor becomes a powder, which is blended with the cocoa butter and other ingredients to make different kinds of chocolate. Plain chocolate is made of cocoa powder, chocolate liquor, cocoa butter and sugar. Milk chocolate, of course, has milk added. White chocolate is made of cocoa butter, milk and sugar. What's missing in white chocolate?

Yes, you've guessed it: the cocoa powder (which would have turned the whole concoction brown).

Britain is the world's biggest consumer of white chocolate, and our most popular white chocolate is the Milky Bar, which was invented by the Swiss firm Nestlé in 1937. It was produced in the company's Hayes factory and it caused a sensation as chocolate-lovers had never before seen or tasted anything like it.

It has been calculated that in Britain 45 white chocolate buttons are eaten every second. That's the equivalent of over 31 million a year. Part of its appeal – especially to parents buying chocolate for their children! – is that white chocolate never causes as much mess when melted as brown does . . .

Do hamsters like going round in those transparent balls?

No they don't. Whoever invented them only considered the interests of the owners and not the hamsters themselves. Yes, hamsters need exercise, but they can get that by going on an exercise wheel in their cage: one which they can get on and off when *they* want to.

We wouldn't like being put in plastic balls – so why do we imagine that hamsters would? It is cruel: they're locked inside and can't get out, and as they run endlessly round and round, they can exhaust themselves and even get heatstroke. True, the hamster balls allow the hamster to be out of its cage and yet safely confined so it doesn't chew the furniture, but there's a big price to pay in terms of hamster welfare. For apart from the problems I've listed above, the balls still allow them to bump into hard surfaces and fall downstairs – in fact, to do all those things that toddlers used to do in baby walkers until they were banned.

Vietnam has banned the sale and possession of hamsters, whose popularity has been soaring. This has nothing to do with animal welfare but because the authorities say the creatures are a potential source of disease. People who want pets are encouraged to have fish instead. The Vietnamese Ministry of Agriculture says anyone caught with a hamster will be fined up to 30 million dong ($1,900) – almost double the average annual wage in Vietnam.

In Australia and New Zealand it is also illegal to keep hamsters as pets but there it's because of the fear that they might escape, breed in the wild and become 'feral' pest animals.

Where does the saying 'no strings attached' come from?

Cloth merchants mark flaws or mistakes in cloth with a tiny white string. Consequently, flawless cloth would have 'no strings attached' and be much more desirable.

That's the derivation of the phrase which has actually come to mean something slightly

different: that a person or a proposition has no drawbacks or ties to anyone or anything else. But then you could see why that would make someone or something more attractive – rather like flawless cloth!

What are the most commonly misspelled words in the English language?

According to surveys, these five words are the most misspelled (a word that is itself frequently misspelled): accommodate, embarrass, grammar, forty and separate.

They're followed by business, harass, necessary, parallel and privilege.

Not far behind these are: all right, calendar, committee, commitment, conscientious, description, existence, government, height, immediately, indispensable, maintenance, occurrence, perseverance, rhythm, seize and transferred.

DIKTIONS
Dictshon
DIKSHUNA
Dictionarry

COMPLETE LIST
OF WORDS ALL
IN ONE BOOK

Would YOU have spelled all these correctly?!

When it comes to pet dogs, what is Britain's most popular breed?

Actually, Britain's favourite dog is the mongrel – which is, of course, a mixture of different breeds. In fact, some mongrels are made up of so many breeds that their owners refer to them affectionately as 'Heinz' – which boasted '57 varieties'.

The most popular specific breed is the Labrador retriever, followed closely by the Yorkshire terrier and the collie.

Why do we call people who are being stupid 'bird-brained'?

The obvious answer is because birds necessarily have very small brains so that they're able to fly. After all, having a big brain would merely weigh them down and make take-off difficult.

According to Charles Watson, a professor of health sciences, 'In almost every language there is a joke about birds, particularly

chickens, being dumb, but in general birds have smarter brains than most mammals – smarter than your average cat or dog. They run rings around dogs, and probably dolphins too. Most birds have incredibly good memories, learning and problem-solving abilities. Chickens can also grasp other complex mental concepts. For instance, chickens are able to understand that objects still exist even after they are hidden or removed from view. This level of cognition is actually beyond the capacity of small human children.'

Researchers have also shown that chickens learn from observing the success and failure of others in their group. One experiment that demonstrated this finding involved teaching one group of chickens to peck red and green buttons a certain number of times to obtain a food reward. Researchers were amazed to find that when a new group of chickens watched those who had learned how to push the buttons for food, they quickly copied what the others had done.

Professor John Webster set up a study in which he gave chickens a mixture of yellow and blue kernels of corn. The blue kernels were tainted with chemicals that made the birds feel sick, and they quickly learned to avoid the blue corn entirely (this is also another example of their understanding of cause and effect). When the chickens in Webster's study had their young, he spread yellow and blue corn around the farm, and even though he made both types harmless, the mother hens remembered that the blue corn had previously made them sick, and they steered their young away from it. Many kinds of bird are so resourceful they are

able to design and manufacture tools, solve mathematical problems and, in many cases, use language in ways that even chimpanzees and other primates cannot.

And if you want proof of that, look at a bird's nest – but only when it's been completely abandoned by the birds. It's an extraordinary feat of construction – made all the more remarkable by the fact that birds don't have hands or fingers but have to rely on their beaks. I doubt very much whether any human could build such a complex structure with their mouth/tongue.

And we can't fly!

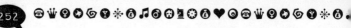
What is a pecking order?

Literally what it says! The order in which chickens – or other birds – will peck at food.

This order is actually very interesting to observe.

You see, chickens are social animals which form really quite complicated hierarchies (i.e. levels of importance).

Watch any group of chickens or just go to your local duck pond and you'll see that they have an order. Every bird knows his or her

place on the social ladder and remembers the faces and rank of up to 100 fellow birds. Just like us, each bird has a different personality, and this is reflected in its place in the order. Some are bold and bossy while others are shy and timid, but there is a definite, structured order, and if a bird fails to observe its place – for example, by pecking at food before its turn – then it will receive a reminder from the other birds.

And what would that reminder be? Yes, you've guessed it . . . a peck! Another reason why it's known as a pecking order!

OK, BIRDS OF PREY FIRST, THEN CHICKENS...

FOOD.

Why do we 'draw' curtains when we open or close them?

It's probably because this is one place where there's no need for two words – open and close.

If the curtains are open and someone asks us to draw them, we can assume that they want us to close them. Similarly, if the curtains are closed and someone asks us to draw them, we can assume that they want us to open them.

It's a rare example of economy in a language that has over a million words.

Is it true you should 'feed a cold' but 'starve a fever'?

According to a doctor I asked, 'When you have fever, your body is working to fight something in your system. You should eat lightly as your body needs energy to digest and it is better to let the body focus on the "fight at hand" and just eat light meals or snacks until the fever breaks, which is usually after a shorter period of time than a common cold.

'On the other hand, your immune system is involved for up to 10 days with a cold. As the system isn't as stressed as it is with flu, there's less need to reduce demands on the digestive system. It makes sense to keep up the supply of healthy vitamins to help make antibodies to defeat the infection. So you eat things that increase their production, such as vitamin C-rich foods and fruit, and soups, and teas, because they add needed fluid, and because warm fluids help to break up the mucus associated with colds.'

Whether you have a cold or a fever, the important thing to remember is to drink plenty of fluids. As long as you are drinking enough water, you can go without food for a few days without coming to any harm.

You're a pretty reasonable chap, Mitch – is there anything that annoys you?

Alas, plenty. Here's a (very) short list:

Female professional tennis players grunting when they hit the ball. Some of them don't just grunt, they squeal as well – '*Ergh-uuuhh!*' – like a sow who's enjoying a meal until, suddenly, her favourite piglet is abducted.

People who borrow your pen and then suck the top.

The Sainsbury's slogan 'Try Something New Today'. All right, I will. I'll go to Waitrose.

Pistachio nuts that can't be opened.

People complaining about the weather in Britain. It's paradise compared to most countries.

Men who wear socks with sandals. Should be against the law. It probably is in Italy.

Unnecessary apostrophe's.

The use in shop names/signs of U instead of 'you' and R instead of 'are'.

TV game-show contestants who clap themselves. They look like seals.

Being told that I bite my nails badly when, in fact, I bite them jolly well.

The words 'New & Improved' on products. If it's new it can't yet be improved.

Footballers taking their shirts off after scoring goals. Why?

Clowns. Very strange.

Junk mail that disguises itself as proper mail. *This requires your immediate attention.* No it doesn't.

Having to buy packs of four batteries for gadgets that require just two.

People who say 'End of' to terminate a conversation.

People who say 'you know' every four or five words.

Men who wear scarves indoors.

Not being sure whether it's scarves or scarfs.

Offal. Awful.

Supermarket trolleys with all four wheels going in different directions.

Any celebrity who describes him- or herself as a 'personality'.

Exaggeratedly pointed shoes (outside of the circus).

People chewing gum with their mouths open.

People who get embarrassed by other people's bad behaviour. This is a peculiarly British condition.

People who say 'fact' at the end of their sentences as though saying that automatically proves them right.

90-second pauses when the results are given in reality TV shows.

Deckchairs. I can't work 'em out – which makes me feel stupid.

Dog poo in parks.

The expression 'How long's a piece of string?'

Actresses playing nurses earning more than real nurses. It's extraordinary when you stop to think about it.

Baseball caps worn backwards.

Public toilets that don't have toilet paper.

Static electricity shocks.

Visible vomit in films and TV dramas.

Chewing gum on the pavement.

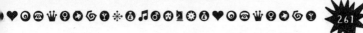

Questions I wasn't able to answer

What if there were no hypothetical questions?

If you tell a joke in the forest, but nobody laughs, was it a joke?

Where does the white go when the snow melts?

Why doesn't Tarzan have a beard?

Why do mums say, 'I'll teach you to behave badly!'

Where do socks go?

What do you call male ballerinas?

Why are our arms too short to scratch the middle of our backs?

Mitchell Symons
HOW MUCH POO DOES AN ELEPHANT DO?*
... and further fascinating facts!

* An elephant produces an eye-wateringly pongy 20 kilograms of dung a day!

Let Mitchell Symons be your guide into the weird and wonderful world of trivia.

- Camels are born without humps
- Walt Disney, creator of Mickey Mouse, was scared of mice
- Only 30% of humans can flare their nostrils
- A group of twelve or more cows is called a flink

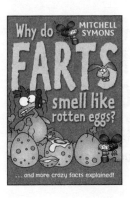

Mitchell Symons
WHY DO FARTS SMELL LIKE ROTTEN EGGS?
... and more crazy facts
explained!

Ever wondered ...

- Why we burp?
- What a wotsit is?
- Whether lemmings really jump off cliffs?
- Why vomit always contains carrots?
- And why *do* farts smell like rotten eggs?

No subject is too strange and no trivia
too tough for Mitchell Symons, who has
the answers to these crazy questions, and
many more.

Q: Who writes the best books on farts, bogeys and other yucky stuff?

A: Mitchell Symons, of course

Q: What's his website called?

A: Grossbooks.co.uk, what else!

On this site you can:
- Win cool stuff in quizzes and competitions
- Add your own fab facts and publish them online
- Be first to find out about Mitchell's new books before they're published

As Mitchell's mum would say:
'Thank goodness it's not *scratch 'n' sniff...*'

See for yourself at **Grossbooks.co.uk**